MOURT'S RELATION

A Journal of the
Pilgrims at Plymouth

MOURT'S RELATION

A Journal of the
Pilgrims at Plymouth

Edited with an introduction and notes by
Dwight B. Heath
from the original text of 1622

Published in cooperation with
Plimoth Plantation, Inc.
Plymouth, Massachusetts

Applewood Books
Bedford, Massachusetts

Mourt's Relation was first published in 1622.

Copyright © 1963 Dwight B. Heath

ISBN: 0-918222-84-2

10 9 8 7

CONTENTS

EDITOR'S INTRODUCTION

Background

The coming of the Pilgrims and their establishment of the Plymouth Plantation is one of the great adventures in the American experience. This book is the earliest published account of that adventure, a day-by-day journal written in a simple forceful manner by men who took part in it. The story is familiar[1]—deceptively familiar, in that portions of it have undergone a complex process of transformation and emerge as modern myths in our national folklore. Still it is a story full of glory, and of tragedy, which deserves a wider public.

The glory, as usual, exists mostly in retrospect. The Separatists had already shown the courage of their convictions in defying both Church and State by worshiping in their own way in England. They had finally been driven to take refuge in Holland, the only European nation where they could then enjoy complete religious tolerance. After twelve years of poverty and social isolation in Amsterdam and Leyden, the self-styled "Saints"[2] sought the New World largely as a land of economic opportunity where they hoped to start afresh. Similiar motives undoubtedly moved the "Strangers,"[3] the motley group of fellow travelers who joined the party at Plymouth, England, and doubled their numbers. The "Strangers" were loyal to the

---

1   An immense body of literature, both popular and scholarly, has been written on the story of the Pilgrims, and much of it is excellent. One of the most comprehensive accounts is also one of the most enjoyable; George F. Willison's *Saints and Strangers* (New York, 1945) combines exhaustive scholarship with style and wit.

2   In the Biblical sense of "God's chosen people," or simply, "members of a Christian church."

3   So-called because they were unknown to members of the Leyden congregation, having been enlisted by the sponsors of the expedition.

Church of England, as were the few indentured servants and hired men, who soon comprised a dissident faction. They cared no more for freedom of conscience than did the "merchant adventurers," a joint stock company of about seventy London businessmen who sponsored the plantation only as a commercial venture likely to yield high profits.

Some have read the "Mayflower Compact" as the glorious cornerstone of American democracy, but it seems hardly revolutionary in context here where it first appeared in print. The fact that the Pilgrims enjoyed warm relations with some Indians is also much to their credit, but it may reflect the charity of the Indians at least as much as their own benevolence. Still one cannot belittle the achievement of these simple people. They consistently showed resourcefulness in coping with new problems, and courage in the face of danger. The greatest glory of the Pilgrims may well have been the ardent faith and dogged persistence which saw them through great tragedy.

Although there is little talk of tragedy in this volume, we know that more than half of the original party died during the first year at Plymouth. Considering their primitive living conditions, it is a wonder that so many did survive the "general sickness" while wading to and from the shallop, and working hard to develop new skills in the harsh and alien environment of a strenuous New England winter. Another tragedy is only presaged here, in the white man's facile rationalization of his usurpation of lands which had long been used by Indians. Within the span of a single lifetime, the indigenous peoples were dispossessed, and their way of life did not long survive after the mutually debilitating "King Philip's War." The tragedy and the glory of Pilgrims and Indians alike emerge in a careful reading of this journal.

About the Book

Any good book must mean many things to many readers, and this journal offers more than just reflections of past glories and intimations of great tragedy. It is a primary source for American history in that critical period when a beach-head of Anglo culture was established in the New World. In this volume are the earliest accounts of the "Mayflower Compact," the establishment of a community which has become focal in our national heritage, the signing of this country's first mutual security pact, and the famous first Thanksgiving. There is no question of the book's essential authenticity, and most of it has the flavor of having been written on the spot at the time.

This sense of immediacy also enhances the value of the journal as a well written story of true adventure. The protagonists quietly suppressed an impending mutiny, even before they landed. While exploring the unknown wastes of Cape Cod, they conducted archeological excavations before they had a roof over their heads. They were attacked by Indians, and yet persisted, built their homes in a foreign land, and soon traveled freely among the natives. This is high adventure indeed!

Political implications are of some importance too. The passengers on the *Mayflower* are famous for their founding of "a civil body politic . . . to enact, constitute, and frame such just and equal laws, ordinances, acts, [and] offices from time to time, as shall be thought most meet and convenient for the general good of the colony." Within less than a week of their first conversation with an Indian, the Pilgrims signed an enduring peace treaty with Massasoit, a leader of the neighboring Wampanoags. A year later, they enjoyed trading relations and military alliance with many other Indian groups.

The journal may also be viewed as a valuable ethnographic document. Although previous sporadic contacts by explorers and traders had yielded some impressionistic descriptions, the Pilgrims were the first Europeans to be in close and sustained contact with the Indians of southern New England. At first they expected only hostility from the "savages," but it was not long before they found valuable helpers in Squanto and Samoset, both of whom had learned already some English when they were kidnapped and sold as slaves by English traders. The Pilgrims were obliged to work out a modus vivendi with these "tall and proper men" whose dress seemed outlandish, whose foods were strange, and whose customs were curious enough to deserve description. We are indebted to the authors of this journal for a wealth of information about such patterns during the brief period before they disappeared forever. There are many aspects of the native ways of life of which the Pilgrims were unaware, and others which they treated with only tantalizing brevity, but a wealth of irreplaceable ethnographic data in this volume serves to illuminate our fragmentary understanding of coastal Algonquian cultures.

Just as we can learn much about the Indians from this book, we can also gain rich insights into the character of the Pilgrims themselves. Mention of the threat of mutiny explodes the hoary myth of dedicated unity of purpose among all members of the party. The bravery of the Pilgrims emerges in bold relief, as does their readiness to rob the graves of Indians. In light of this text, their industriousness cannot be doubted. Flashes of humor occur, and their strong sense of being a "chosen people" is clearly manifest in recurrent references to a felicitous "divine providence."

"Human interest" is not lacking either. We can imagine the chagrin of William Bradford unwittingly caught up in a deer snare, just as we can sympathize with the consternation created when a prankish boy fired his father's musket in a ship's cabin where open kegs of gunpowder lay about. It is easy to feel for the "old [Indian] woman whom we judged to be no less than a hundred years old" who wept because "she was deprived of the comfort of her children in her old age" when Capt. Hunt kidnapped her three sons. And how his playmates must have envied the boy who was lost on Cape Cod, and was returned by the Nauset Indians, "behung with beads"!

Within this brief but diverse book there is also a pervasive mystery, for no one knows who wrote it. The book has become known as *Mourt's Relation*, but it is not the unitary effort of a single man. Five of the ten "chapters" have bylines, and Mourt's contribution is almost the briefest of the ten. The mystery deepens when we confess not knowing much about the man named Mourt. Perhaps the most fruitful way to approach the problem is through a discussion of the several components of the book.

It opens with a dedicatory letter of transmittal "To his much respected friend. . . ." This is a form of profuse and discursive acknowledgment typical of the time. It seems to have been appended by an associate of the settlers, whose concern was ". . . but the recommendation of the relation itself," to a distinguished member of the "merchant adventurers" who had sponsored the *Mayflower* voyage. The dedication is signed *R.G.,* which I assume to be a misprint for the initials of Robert Cushman. The only member of the party at Plymouth with initials R.G. was Richard Gardiner, an undistinguished "Stranger" who stayed only briefly and took little part in the venture. The fact that misprints are frequent throughout the rest of the book suggests the possibility of reference to Cushman, who is a person most likely to have drafted such a letter. As a deacon of the Leyden congregation who also served as their business agent, he was instrumental in securing English permission for removal to the New World, and, after having had to turn back on the unseaworthy *Speedwell,* he continued negotiations with the "merchant adventurers" while the *Mayflower* sailed on to Plymouth. Visiting the plantation on the second ship, *Fortune,* he delivered the patent which confirmed their legal right to settle there, together with a stringent contract from the sponsors, which he finally induced the Pilgrims to sign, after preaching a pointed sermon on "The Dangers of Self-Love." The manuscript of the relations must have been carried back to England with him on the *Fortune* in December of 1621.

Appended at the end of the volume is another chapter which I attribute to Cushman. A long exposition of "Reasons and considerations touching the lawfulness of removing out of England into the parts of America," signed *R.C.,* is a thinly veiled promotional tract organized like a sermon, which cites Scripture to justify the plantation and to persuade others to follow.

Among the prefatory letters is one containing "Certain useful advertisements . . ." and signed *I.R.*. We are told that this letter of advice concerning man's proper relation with God and with his fellow men was ". . . written by a discreet friend unto the planters in New England, at their first setting sail from Southampton."[4] This "unfeigned well-willer" is most likely John Robinson, pastor of the expatriate Separatist congregation in Leyden, and hence understandably solicitous for the welfare of the Pilgrims, and also in a position to proffer such counsel. The letter may have been appended to this book especially to serve as a model of morality for those "Strangers" who might hopefully be induced to emigrate and join the party at Plymouth.

Five "relations" constitute the major portion of the book, and none of these is signed. The first and longest, on "The proceedings of the plantation . . .," begins with the departure from Plymouth, England, and recounts events of the next six months, including the voyage, the signing of the "compact," the several "discoveries," the choice of a site and the building there, as well as early contacts with the Indians, culminating in the signing of a peace treaty with Massasoit. A second deals with "A journey to Pokanoket . . ." and describes further friendly dealings with the Wampanoag Indians. The next treats "A voyage . . . to the Kingdom of Nauset, to seek a boy that had lost himself in the woods. . . ." An account of "A journey to Nemasket . . ." shows how the Pilgrims sought to defend their Indian allies against the hostile Narragansets, and "A relation of our voyage to the Massachusets . . ." describes the expansion of trade relations to the north.

According to the dedicatory letter, these vivid reports were ". . . writ by the several actors themselves, after their plain and

4 The Pilgrims originally embarked in two ships at Southampton, 5 August 1620, but because the *Speedwell* leaked dangerously they put in at Dartmouth for repairs. When they returned to the open sea, they discovered that she still shipped water. Turning to the nearest port, they reluctantly decided to aban-don the *Speedwell* as unseaworthy, and many of the party transferred to the already crowded *Mayflower*, while a few decided to defer their emigration. The successful voyage from Plymouth began 6 September, with their third departure from the homeland.

rude manner." It is almost certain that the principal author was Edward Winslow, although it is generally believed that William Bradford also had a hand in the effort. Both of these men were among the few who were prominent in the affairs of the plantation, and they two are the only ones of the first party who obviously enjoyed writing. Winslow's *Good News from New England* (London, 1624), continued the narrative of the plantation from the time when this volume left off, and is markedly similar in style. In his *Good News . . .*, Winslow mentions descriptions of aspects of Indian culture which were prepared by ". . . myself and others, in former letters, (which came to the press against my will and knowledge) . . ."; I know of no publication other than *Mourt's Relation* to which this could refer. Bradford's manuscript history *Of Plymouth Plantation* (first published in Boston, 1856) has become the principal source on the Pilgrim experience, although he could hardly be said to claim priority when he ". . . first began these scribbled writings (which was about the year 1630 and so pieced up at times of leisure afterward)." His treatment of the first year at Plymouth is a curious combination, consisting largely of passages identical with those in *Mourt's Relation,* together with discursive classical allusions and philosophic ruminations. Bradford's style generally tends to be more analytic than descriptive, and the specificity of detail which makes this text such a rich source material for the historian and ethnographer rarely occurs elsewhere in Bradford's work. It is entirely within the realm of possibility that he may have incorporated in his manuscript the work of others as it had appeared in *Mourt's Relation;* he freely adopted material from other sources.

The ensuing "Letter sent from New England . . . setting forth . . . the worth of that plantation . . .," follows the five narrative relations closely in style, and is signed by *E.W.*. It is almost certainly Winslow who here sounds vaguely like a twentieth-century Florida real estate agent when he describes the first Thanksgiving as indicating the richness of the land: "I never in my life remember a more seasonable year than we have here enjoyed and if we have once but kine, horses, and sheep, I make no question but men might live as contented here as in any part of the world." He also includes some very specific suggestions concerning the practical needs of those who might choose to come.

And what was Mourt's contribution to the book which has been linked with his name by historians, librarians, and bibliographers since Prince[5] first invented the convenient title, *Mourt's Relation,* as a substitute for the cumbersome original? A brief foreword, or introduction, "To the reader," is all that we must credit to the signer, one *G. Mourt.* It may have been he who was responsible for bringing to press this collection of papers, ". . . hoping of a cheerful proceeding, both of adventurers and planters." He explicitly denied authorship of the narratives: "These relations coming to my hand from my both known and faithful friends, on whose writings I do much rely, I thought it not amiss to make them more general. . . ." But scholars still do not know who he was!

It is suggested that he had at some time been associated with the authors of the relations, whom he called "my both known and faithful friends." It is also suggested that he had long hoped to emigrate to the New World, ". . . as myself then much desired, and shortly hope to effect, if the Lord will, the putting to of my shoulder in this hopeful business." These criteria clearly apply to Robert Cushman, who, as we have seen, was a person who might appropriately have introduced such a book.

The specifications also apply to another member of the Leyden congregation who was active in negotiating with the "merchant adventurers" until he did sail to Plymouth, on the first ship bound for the plantation after the book was printed. If no more than the initials had been given in the signature to the introduction—as was the case in every other portion of the volume—there would be little hesitation to identify the author as George Morton.

5   Thomas Prince, *A Chronological History of New England* . . . (Boston, 1736), vol. 1, pt. 2, p. 71, fn. 38.

As it is, however, one must attempt to account for the discrepancy in name if he suggests that it may have been Morton who wrote it. It is easy to suggest that the use of "Mourt" for "Morton" could have been merely another of the many misprints in the book. At least as plausible, however, is the suggestion that it may have been a pseudonym. It is not difficult to imagine why there might have been some attempt to conceal the fact *if* Morton had been intimately involved in the preparation and promulgation of the book. A printer might have been reluctant to "publish" a document written by Separatists unless it carried an introduction by an apparently disinterested party. In a period of strict royal control of the press in England, William Brewster of the Leyden congregation had already incurred the wrath of King James by printing an outspoken opposition tract, *Perth Assembly* (Leyden, 1619), so that any writings by his friends and associates might logically also be suspect. Furthermore, the fact that *Mourt's Relation* is essentially a promotional effort is clearly implied in the phrasing of the original title, describing the "safe arrival" of the "English planters," and "their joyful building of, and comfortable planting themselves in the now well defended town of New Plymouth." In such an effort to excite more prospective settlers, it would have been sound public relations to minimize the degree of identification between the plantation and the "Saints," who were popularly scorned as heretics and criminals.

Another possibility must be mentioned. I am only half-joking when I suggest that at least this portion of *Mourt's Relation* may actually have been written by someone named G. Mourt, of whom we know nothing else. One of the delights of historical research is the fact that one always raises more questions than he can answer. The mystery remains.

Mourt's Relation is clearly a book which offers different meanings to every reader. I hope that this edition may reach a broad audience and increase popular understanding of a neglected portion of the American experience.

EDITOR'S INTRODUCTION

A Note on This Edition

My intention is to provide the contemporary reader with an appreciation of this exciting book as it was received by an eager and curious public when it was first published almost three and a half centuries ago. In keeping with this aim, the entire text is included here, in the order of the original.[6] So that the authors may speak forcefully and directly to the reader of today, I have introduced only uniform spelling, punctuation, and paragraphing, structural niceties which were of no concern to authors or printers until late in the eighteenth century. The eloquent English language of the period is familiar to us all, through the King James version of the Bible or the works of Shakespeare, and I have scrupuously left each word intact. The text, then, is reproduced verbatim, including marginalia, chapter headings, and running heads, altered only by the use of modern orthography for the sake of clarity.

I have deliberately avoided distracting the reader from the original text, by introducing a minimum of footnotes. Some annotation seems indispensable for understanding the work of another age, but this edition does not bear the tender burden of scholarly disquisition. Modern equivalents are given for archaic words and place-names, and I have offered brief explanations of a few outdated allusions. Dates are retained as in the original, so that ten days must be added to any date given in the text in order to fit it into the modern Gregorian calendar, which was not adopted by England and her colonies until 1752.

6 Although portions of the book have been reprinted frequently, the only other presentation of the full text was a facsimile in an edition limited to 285 copies, prepared by Henry M. Dexter, and entitled *Mourt's Relation* (Boston, 1865). It is a heavily annotated volume, and Dexter's monumental effort has aided a generation of scholars, but his meticulous attention to "faithful reproduction of the original, letter for letter" makes it formidable to any but a dedicated student. The best known and most widely available edition includes annotation and uniform spelling, but is marred by some minor omissions and transpositions: Alexander Young, *Chronicles of the Pilgrim Fathers* (Boston, 1841), pp. 110-249.

EDITOR'S INTRODUCTION

In the exacting task of collating this text with the original, I was helped by my friend and colleague, Anna Mae Cooper. We worked in the John Carter Brown Library where Thomas R. Adams kindly put excellent facilities at our disposal, including the library's copy of the first edition of the book, as well as the Smith and Champlain maps. Lucille Hanna first introduced me to the excitement of history, and J. L. Giddings pointed out the ethnographic value of *Mourt's Relation*. Miss Rose T. Briggs, Director of Pilgrim Hall, shared her enthusiasm and broad knowledge of the Pilgrims. E. Lawrence Couter, David Freeman, Arthur G. Pyle, Muriel Stefani, and the entire staff of Plimoth Plantation were helpful in many ways, and the corporation generously provided the photographs. The title page, ornamental letters and top-page designs are reproduced from a copy of the original, now in possession of the Rhode Island Historical Society. Mrs. N. Mac Donald typed from a difficult manuscript.

An adventure such as this rightfully belongs to all who would chase rainbows!

DWIGHT B. HEATH
Brown University
Providence, R. I.

SAMUEL DE CHAMPLAIN'S MAP OF PLYMOUTH HARBOR

Although the Pilgrims were the first Europeans to establish a permanent colony in northeastern North America, they did not come to an unknown land. As early as 1605, Samuel de Champlain had mapped Plymouth Harbor, in the course of a three-year expedition during which he explored the coast from Nova Scotia to Martha's Vineyard. The quality of his detailed and accurate observations on the land and people appears in this map, and in his notes on the visit: "There came to us two or three canoes, which had just been fishing for cod and other fish which are found there in large numbers. These they catch with hooks made of a piece of wood, to which they attach a bone in the shape of a spear and fasten it very securely. The whole has a fang-shape, and the line attached to it is made out of the bark of a tree. They gave me one of their hooks, which I took out of curiosity. In it the bone was fastened on by hemp, like that in France, as it seemed to me, and they told me that they gathered this plant without being obliged to cultivate it, and indicated that it grew to the height of four or five feet. This canoe went back on shore to give notice to their fellow inhabitants, who caused columns of smoke to arise on our account. We saw eighteen or twenty savages, who came to the shore and began to dance. Our canoe landed in order to give them some bagatelles, at which they were greatly pleased. Some of them came to us and begged us to go to their river. We weighed anchor to do so, but but were unable to enter on account of the small amount of water, it being low tide, and were accordingly obliged to anchor at the mouth. I went ashore, where I saw many others, who received us very cordially. I made also an examination of the river, but saw only an arm of water extending a short distance inland, where the land is only in part cleared. Running into this is merely a brook not deep enough for boats except at full tide. The circuit of the bay is about a league. On one side of the entrance to this bay there is a point which is almost an island, covered with wood, principally pines, and adjoins sandbanks, which are very extensive. On the other side, the land is high. There are two islets in this bay, which are not seen until one has entered, and around which it is almost entirely dry at low tide. This place is very conspicuous from the sea, for the coast is very low, excepting the cape at the entrance to the bay. We named it the Port du Cap. St. Louis . . .".

Reproduced is a copy from a first edition of *Les Voyages du Sieur de Champlain* (Paris, 1613), now in possession of the John Carter Brown Library.

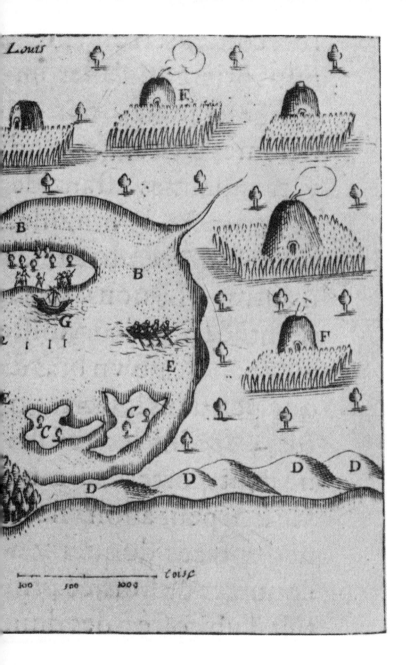

CAPTAIN JOHN SMITH'S MAP OF NEW ENGLAND

The Pilgrims were familiar with Capt. John Smith's account of a voyage in which he had surveyed the coast from Cape Cod to Penobscot Bay in 1614. He had even offered his services as guide and military captain, but Myles Standish got the job. Undoubtedly they did bring with them his *Description of New England* (London, 1616), in which the following map was published.

Capt. Smith, who had already gained some fame and fortune in Virginia, dedicated to Prince Charles this effort in which the term "New England" first appeared: ". . . it being my chance to range some other parts of America, whereof I here present your highness the description in a map, my humble suit [in original, "sure"] is you would please to change their barbarous names for such English, as posterity may say Prince Charles was their godfather." Several English place-names were incorporated in the map, but posterity disregarded most of them, a noteworthy exception being "Plimouth." Smith notes that the Indians called the site ". . . Accomack, an excellent good harbor, good land, and no want of any thing but industrious people," recalling that "After much kindness, upon a small occasion we fought also with 40 or 50 of those [Indians]; though some were hurt and some slain, yet within an hour after, they became friends."

The map was subsequently reissued in several other works by Smith, additions being made on the engraved copper plate from time to time, to indicate more recent discoveries and settlements. The copy reproduced here is from a first edition, now in possession of the John Carter Brown Library; obviously the representations of European-style buildings were as inappropriate as were the illustrations of monsters, introduced by imaginatively artistic cartographers. (The note concerning Smith's death was written in ink by a previous owner of this copy.)

NEW ENG

The most remarqueable parts thus
by the high and mighty Prince C
Prince of great Britaine

THE PORTRAICTUER OF CAPTAYNE IOHN SMITH ADMIRALL OF NEW ENGLAND.

Æ̃tat 37
A⁰ 1616

These are the Lines that shew thy Face, but those
That shew thy Grace and Glory, brighter bee
Thy Faire-Discoueries and Fowle-Overthrowes
Of Salvages, much Civillizd by thee
Best shew thy Spirit; and to it Glory Wynn;
So, thou art Brasse without, but Golde within.

If so, in Brasse (too soft Smiths Acts to beare)
I fix thy Fame, to make Brasse Steele out weare.
Thine as thou art Vertues,
John Davies Heref:

Schooters hill
Sandwich
Dartmouth
Jswich
Snadoun hill
Eston
Hull
Poynt Dauies
Smith Iles
South-Hampton
Bristow
Cape ANNA
Talbotts Bay
Fawmouth
Fullerton Ils
The River CHARLES
Cary Ils
Cheuyot hills
P. Murry
London
Oxford
Poynt Sutliff
Poynt Gorge
Cape IAMES
Plimouth
STUARDS Bay
Barwich

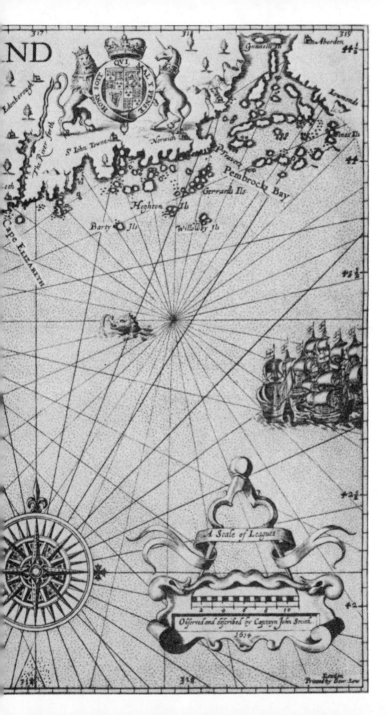

ND

HONI SOIT QVI MALY PENSE

QVI

Edenborough

The River Forth

St John Towne

Norwich

Cape Elizabeth

Heghton Ils

Barty Ils

Willowby Ils

Gerrards Ils

Piratery see Pembrocke Bay

Gunnells Hil

Aborden

Lowmonds

Snes Ils

A Scale of Leagues

Observed and described by Captayn John Smith.
1614

London
Printed by Dow Low

A
RELATION OR

Iournall of the beginning and proceedings
of the English Plantation setled at *Plimoth* in NEW
ENGLAND, by certaine English Aduenturers both
Merchants and others.

With their difficult passage, their safe ariuall, their
ioyfull building of, and comfortable planting them-
selues in the now well defended Towne
of NEW PLIMOTH.

AS ALSO A RELATION OF FOVRE
seuerall discoueries since made by some of the
same English Planters there resident.

I. In a iourney to PVCKANOKICK *the habitation of the Indians greatest King* Massasoyt : *as also their message, the answer and entertainment
they had of him.*

II. In a voyage made by ten of them to the Kingdome of Nawset, *to seeke
a boy that had lost himselfe in the woods : with such accidents as befell them
in that voyage.*

III. In their iourney to the Kingdome of Namascnet, *in defence of their
greatest King* Massasoyt, *against the* Narrohiggonsets, *and to reuenge the
supposed death of their Interpreter* Tisquantum.

IIII. Their voyage to the Massachusets, *and their entertainment there.*

With an answer to all such obiections as are any way made
against the lawfulnesse of English plantations
in those parts.

LONDON,
Printed for *Iohn Bellamie*, and are to be sold at his shop at the two
Greyhounds in Cornhill neere the Royall Exchange, 1622.

A
RELATION OR
Journal of the beginning and proceedings
of the English Plantation settled at *Plymouth* in New
England, by certain English adventurers both
merchants and others.
With their difficult passage, their safe arrival, their
joyful building of, and comfortable planting themselves in the now well defended town
of New Plymouth

AS ALSO A RELATION OF FOUR
several discoveries since made by some of the
same English Planters there resident.

I. *In a journey to* Pokanoket, *the habitation of the Indians' greatest King* Massasoit: *as also their message, the answer and entertainment they had of him.*

II. *In a voyage made by ten of them to the Kingdom of* Nauset, *to seek a boy that had lost himself in the wood: with such accidents as befell them in that voyage.*

III. *In their journey to the Kingdom of* Nemasket, *in defense of their greatest King* Massasoit, *against the* Narragansets, *and to revenge the supposed death of their Interpreter* Squanto.

IIII. *Their voyage to the* Massachusets, *and their entertainment there.*

With an answer to all such objections as are any way made
against the lawfulness of English plantations
in those parts.

LONDON,
Printed for *John Bellamie,* and are to be sold at his shop
at the Two Greyhounds in Cornhill near the Royal Exchange. 1622.

TO HIS MUCH
respected friend, Mr. I. P.[1]

 Ood Friend: ·

As we cannot but account it an extraordinary blessing of God in directing our course for these parts, after we came out of our native country, for that we had the happiness to be possessed of the comforts we receive by the benefit of one of the most pleasant, most healthful, and most fruitful parts of the world; so must we acknowledge the same blessing to be multiplied upon our whole company, for that we obtained the honor to receive allowance and approbation of our free possession and enjoying thereof, under the authority of those thrice honored persons, the President and

1 Presumably, the initials of John Peirce. Peirce was a London businessman one of the "merchant adventurers" who had contributed to the *Mayflower's* first voyage. It is possible that he underwrote the printing of the book; it is certain that the patent to lands occupied by the Pilgrims — as virtual squatters for almost a year — was finally issued in his name, in trust for the settlers. They were delighted to receive this confirmation of their legal rights, and may have dedicated the book to him in gratitude. Only later did they learn of the many devious ways in which he tried to cheat them.

3

Council for the Affairs of New England, by whose bounty and grace, in that behalf, all of us are tied to dedicate our best service unto them,[2] as those under his Majesty, that we owe it unto, whose noble endeavors in these their actions the God of heaven and earth multiply to his glory and their own eternal comforts.

As for this poor relation, I pray you to accept it, as being writ by the several actors themselves, after their plain and rude manner; therefore doubt nothing of the truth thereof. If it be defective in any thing, it is their ignorance, that are better acquainted with planting than writing. If it satisfy those that are well affected to the business, it is all I care for. Sure I am the place we are in, and the hopes that are apparent, cannot but suffice any that will not desire more than enough. Neither is there want of aught among us but company to enjoy the blessings so plentifully bestowed upon the inhabitants that are here. While I was a-writing this, I had almost forgot that I had but the recommendation of the relation itself to your further con-

2 Acknowledging their indebtedness to Sir Ferdinando Gorges and his partners in the Council for New England, (formerly, the Second Virginia Company, and the Plymouth Company), who exercised legal authority over the area, which had previously been called "Northern Virginia."

4

sideration, and therefore I will end without saying more, save that I shall always rest

Yours in the way of friendship,

R. G.[3]

From Plymouth, in New England.

---

3 Presumably a misprint for the initials of Robert Cushman. See Introduction.

To the Reader

Ourteous Reader, be entreated to make a favorable construction of my forwardness in publishing these ensuing discourses. The desire of carrying the Gospel of Christ into those foreign parts, amongst those people that as yet have had no knowledge nor taste of God, as also to procure unto themselves and others a quiet and comfortable habitation, were, amongst other things, the inducements (unto these undertakings of the then hopeful, and now experimentally known good enterprise for plantation in New England) to set afoot and prosecute the same. And though it fared with them, as it is common to the most actions of this nature, that the first attempts prove difficult, as the sequel more at large expresseth, yet it hath pleased God, even beyond our expectation in so short a time, to give hope of letting some of them see (though some he hath taken out of this vale of tears)[1] some grounds of hope of the accomplishment of both those ends by them at first propounded.

1 The writer studiously avoids mentioning the grim fact that more than half of the group who sailed on the *Mayflower* had already died.

*And as myself then much desired, and short-
ly hope to effect, if the Lord will, the putting
to of my shoulder in this hopeful business, and
in the meantime, these relations coming to my
hand from my both known and faithful
friends, on whose writings I do much rely, I
thought it not amiss to make them more general,
hoping of a cheerful proceeding, both of adventurers and planters, entreating that the ex-
ample of the honorable Virginia and Bermudas
Companies, encountering with so many disas-
ters, and that for divers years together, with an
unwearied resolution, the good effects whereof
are now eminent, may prevail as a spur of preparation also touching this no less hopeful country, though yet an infant, the extent and commodities whereof are as yet not fully known,
after time will unfold more. Such as desire
to take knowledge of things, may inform themselves by this ensuing treatise, and, if they
please, also by such as have been there a first
and second time.[2] My hearty prayer to God is*

2 Although they were pioneer settlers in New England, the Pilgrims had not come to unknown territory. This portion of the
   coast had been sailed by Giovanni de Verrazzano as early as
   1524; probably the first Englishman to visit the area was Bar-
   tholomew Gosnold in 1602. In 1605, George Waymouth commanded a voyage of exploration and trade, and kipnapped five
   Indians in Maine, of whom one, Squanto, later befriended the
   Pilgrims. By 1608, Samuel de Champlain had even charted
   the *Port du Cap de St. Louis,* which was to become Plymouth
   Harbor. Capt. John Smith's map of New England, prepared on
   a voyage in 1614, already shows the site named "Plimouth."
   Apparently two mates (or pilots?) of the *Mayflower* had sailed
   the coast previously.

that the event of this and all other honorable and honest undertakings, may be for the furtherance of the kingdom of Christ, the enlarging of the bounds of our sovereign lord King James, and the good and profit of those who, either by purse or person or both, are agents in the same, so I take leave, and rest

Thy friend,

G. Mourt.[3]

---

3 Reasons for assuming that the writer is George Morton have been discussed in the Introduction.

CERTAIN USEFUL
ADVERTISEMENTS SENT
in a Letter written by a discreet friend unto the
Planters in New England, at their first setting
sail from Southampton, who earnestly desireth
the prosperity of that their new
Plantation.

Oving and Christian friends, I do
heartily and in the Lord salute you all,
as being they with whom I am present
in my best affection, and most earnest
longings after you, though I be constrained for a while to be bodily absent from you; I
say constrained, God knowing how willingly and
much rather than otherwise I would have borne my
part with you in this first brunt, were I not by strong
necessity held back for the present. Make account
of me in the meanwhile, as of a man divided in
myself with great pain, and as (natural bonds set
aside) having my better part with you.

And though I doubt not but in your godly wisdoms
you both foresee and resolve upon that which concerneth your present state and condition, both

9

severally and jointly, yet have I thought but my duty to add some further spur of provocation unto them who run already, if not because you need it, yet because I owe it in love and duty.

And first, as we are daily to renew our repentance with our God, special for our sins known, and general for our unknown trespasses, so doth the Lord call us in a singular manner upon occasions of such difficulty and danger as lieth upon you, to a both more narrow search and careful reformation of our ways in his sight, lest he, calling to remembrance our sins forgotten by us or unrepented of, take advantage against us, and in judgment leave us for the same to be swallowed up in one danger or other; whereas on the contrary, sin being taken away by earnest repentance and pardon thereof from the Lord, sealed up unto a man's conscience by his Spirit, great shall be his security and peace in all dangers, sweet his comforts in all distresses, with happy deliverance from all evil, whether in life or in death.

Now next after this heavenly peace with God and our own consciences, we are carefully to provide for peace with all men what in us lieth, especially with our associates, and for that end watchfulness must be had, that we neither at all in ourselves do give, no, nor easily take offense being given by others. Woe be unto the world for offenses, for though it be necessary (considering the malice of Satan and man's corruption) that offenses come, yet woe unto the man or woman either by whom the offense cometh, saith Christ, Matt. 18:7. And if offenses in the unseasonable use of things in themselves indifferent, be more to be feared than death itself, as the Apostle teacheth, 1 Cor. 9:15, how much more in things simply evil, in which neither honor of God, nor love of man is thought worthy to be regarded.

Neither yet is it sufficient that we keep ourselves by the grace of God from giving offense, except withal we be armed against the taking of them when they are given by others. For how unperfect and lame is the work of grace in that person, who wants charity to cover a multitude of offenses, as the Scriptures speak. Neither are you to be exhorted to this grace only upon the common grounds of Christianity, which are, that persons ready to take offense, either want charity to cover offenses, or wisdom duly to weigh human frailty; or lastly are gross, though close hypocrites, as Christ our Lord teacheth, Matt. 7:1,2,3, as indeed in mine own experience, few or none have been found which sooner give offense, than such as easily take it; neither have they ever proved sound and profitable members in societies, which have nourished in themselves that touchy humor.

But besides these, there are divers special motives provoking you above others to great care and conscience this way: as first, you are many of you strangers, as to the persons, so to the infirmities one of another, and so stand in need of more watchfulness this way, lest when such things fall out in men and women as you suspected not, you be inordinately affected with them, which doth require at your hands much wisdom and charity for the covering and preventing of incident offenses that way. And lastly your intended course of civil community will minister continual occasion of offense, and will be as fuel for that fire, except you diligently quench it with brotherly forbearance. And if taking offense causelessly or easily at men's doings be so carefully to be avoided, how much more heed is to be taken that we take not offense at God himself, which yet we certainly do so oft as we do murmur at his providence in our crosses, or bear impatiently such afflictions as wherewith he pleaseth to visit us. Store we up therefore patience against the evil day, without which we take offense at the Lord himself in his holy and just works.

A fourth thing there is carefully to be provided for, to wit, that with your common employments you join common affections truly bent upon the general good, avoiding as a deadly plague of your both common and special comfort all retiredness of mind for proper advantage, and all singularly affected any manner of way; let every man repress in himself and the whole body in each person, as so many rebels against the common good, all private respects of men's selves, not sorting with the general conveniency. And as men are careful not to have a new house shaken with any violence before it be well settled and the parts firmly knit, so be you, I beseech you brethren, much more careful, that the house of God which you are and are to be, be not shaken with unnecessary novelties or other oppositions at the first settling thereof.

Lastly, whereas you are to become a body politic, using amongst yourselves civil government, and are not furnished with any persons of special eminency above the rest, to be chosen by you into office of government, let your wisdom and godliness appear not only in choosing such persons as do entirely love, and will diligently promote the common good, but also in yielding unto them all due honor and obedience in their lawful administrations, not beholding in them the ordinariness of their persons, but God's ordinance for your good, nor being like unto the foolish multitude, who more honor the gay coat than either the virtuous mind of the man or glorious ordinance of the Lord. But you know better things, and that the image of the Lord's power and authority which the Magistrate beareth is honorable, in how mean persons soever. And this duty you both may the more willingly, and ought the more conscionably to perform, because you are at least for the present to have only them for your ordinary governors which yourselves shall make choice of for that work.

Sundry other things of importance I could put you in mind of, and of those before mentioned in more words, but I will not so far wrong your godly minds as to think you heedless of these things, there being also divers among you so well able to admonish both themselves and others of what concerneth them.

These few things therefore, and the same in few words I do earnestly commend unto your care and conscience, joining therewith my daily incessant prayers unto the Lord, that he who hath made the heavens and the earth, the sea and all rivers of waters, and whose providence is over all his works, especially over all his dear children for good, would so guide and guard you in your ways, as inwardly by his Spirit, so outwardly by the hand of his power, as that both you and we also, for and with you, may have after matter of praising his name all the days of your and our lives. Fare you well in him in whom you trust, and in whom I rest

An unfeigned well-willer
of your happy success
in this hopeful voyage,

I. R.[1]

---

1 Presumably, the initials of John Robinson, pastor of the Leyden congregation. See Introduction.

A RELATION OR JOURNAL
OF THE PROCEEDINGS
OF THE PLANTATION
settled at Plymouth
in New England.

Ednesday, the sixth of September, the wind coming east-north-east, a fine small gale, we loosed from Plymouth, having been kindly entertained and courteously used by divers friends there dwelling, and after many difficulties in boisterous storms, at length, by God's providence, upon the ninth of November following, by break of the day we espied land which we deemed to be Cape Cod, and so afterward it proved. And the appearance of it much comforted us, especially seeing so goodly a land, and wooded to the brink of the sea. It caused us to rejoice together, and praise God that had given us once again to see land. And thus we made our course south-south-west, purposing to go to a river ten leagues to the south of the Cape,[1] but at night the wind being contrary, we put round again for the bay of Cape Cod. And upon the 11th of November we came to an anchor in the bay,[2] which is a good harbor and pleasant bay, circled round, except in the entrance which is about four miles over from land to land, compassed about to the very sea with oaks, pines, juniper, sassafras, and other sweet wood. It is a harbor wherein a thousand sail of ships may safely ride. There we relieved ourselves with wood and water, and refreshed our people, while our shallop was fitted to coast the bay, to search for a habitation. There was the greatest store of fowl that ever we saw.

And every day we saw whales playing hard by us, of which in that place, if we had instruments and means to take them, we might have made a very rich return, which to our great grief we wanted. Our master and his mate, and others experienced in fishing, professed we might have made three or four thousand pounds' worth of oil. They preferred it before Greenland whale-fishing, and purpose the next winter to fish for whale here. For cod we assayed, but found none; there is good store, no doubt, in their season. Neither got we any fish all the time we lay there, but some few little ones on the shore. We found great mussels, and very fat and full of sea-pearl, but we could not eat them, for they made us all sick that did eat, as well sailors as passengers. They caused to cast and scour,[3] but they were soon well again.

The bay is so round and circling that before we could come to anchor we went round all the points of the com-

1 Bradford's *Of Plymouth Plantation* identifies this as the Hudson River, where the New Netherlands Company had invited the Pilgrims to settle. Ten leagues appears too short a distance from Cape Cod to the Hudson: *ten* may here be a misprint, or reference may be to the appropriate latitude rather than to the mouth of the river.
2 Presumably, Provincetown Harbor.
3 to vomit and have diarrhea

pass. We could not come near the shore by three quarters of an English mile, because of shallow water, which was a great prejudice to us, for our people going on shore were forced to wade a bow shot or two in going a land, which caused many to get colds and coughs, for it was nigh times freezing cold weather.

This day before we came to harbor, observing some not well affected to unity and concord, but gave some appearance of faction,[4] it was thought good there should be an association and agreement that we should combine together in one body, and to submit to such government and governors as we should by common consent agree to make and choose, and set our hands to this that follows word for word.[5]

In the name of God, Amen. We whose names are underwritten, the loyal subjects of our dread sovereign lord King James, by the grace of God, of Great Britain, France, and Ireland King, Defender of the Faith, etc.

Having undertaken, for the glory of God, and advancement of the Christian faith, and honor of our king and country, a voyage to plant the first colony in the northern

4 Members of the Leyden congregation were fearful of mutiny and other abuses by some of the many "Strangers" who had joined the group in England. The party had no patent for New England, so that they would have been a people outside the law as soon as they disembarked, and individual license could have posed a real threat.

5 The following is the earliest know text of the famous "Mayflower Compact", the original document has never been found. John Quincy Adams overstated the case when he said that "This is perhaps the only instance in human history of that positive social compact which speculative philosophers have imagined as the only legitimate source of government." As evidenced in the signatures, the distinction between masters and servants remained, and women had no legal voice but were still chattel. Nevertheless, it is an unusual document in which the concept of self-government emerges so sharply during a time when the divine right of kings was assumed. It is clearly modelled on the "covenants" or "combinations" which characterized most Separatist congregations, and is presaged in Rev. Robinson's farewell letter.

parts of Virginia, do by these presents solemnly and mutually in the presence of God and one of another, covenant, and combine ourselves together into a civil body politic, for our better ordering and preservation, and furtherance of the ends aforesaid; and by virtue hereof to enact, constitute, and frame such just and equal laws, ordinances, acts, constitutions, offices from time to time, as shall be thought most meet and convenient for the general good of the colony: unto which we promise all due submission and obedience. In witness whereof we have hereunder subscribed our names; Cape Cod, the 11th of November, in the year of the reign of our sovereign lord King James, of England, France and Ireland eighteenth and of Scotland fifty-fourth, Anno Domini 1620.[6]

The same day, so soon as we could we set ashore fifteen or sixteen men, well armed, with some to fetch wood, for we had none left; as also to see what the land was, and what inhabitants they could meet with. They found it to be a small neck of land, on this side where we lay is the bay, and the further side the sea; the ground or earth, sand hills, much like the downs in Holland, but much better; the crust of the earth a spit's[7] depth excellent black earth; all wooded with oaks, pines, sassafras, juniper, birch, holly, vines, some ash, walnut; the wood for the most part

6 The names of the signers were first printed in Nathaniel Morton's *New England's Memorial* (Cambridge, 1669). In alphabetical order, they are:
John Alden, Isaac Allerton, John Allerton, John Billington, William Bradford, William Brewster, Richard Britteridge, Peter Brown, John Carver, James Chilton, Richard Clark, Francis Cook, John Crackstone, Edward Doten, Francis Eaton, Thomas English, Moses Fletcher, Edward Fuller, Samuel Fuller, Richard Gardiner, John Goodman, Stephen Hopkins, John Howland, Edward Leister, Edmond Margeson, Christopher Martin, William Mullins, Digory Priest, John Ridgedale, Thomas Rogers, George Soule, Miles Standish, Edward Tilley, John Tilley, Thomas Tinker, John Turner, Richard Warren, William White, Thomas Williams, Edward Winslow, Gilbert Winslow.
7 spade's

open and without underwood, fit either to go or ride in. At night our people returned, but found not any person, nor habitation, and laded their boat with juniper, which smelled very sweet and strong and of which we burnt the most part of the time we lay there.

Monday, the 13th of November, we unshipped our shallop[8] and drew her on land, to mend and repair her, having been forced to cut her down in bestowing her betwixt the decks, and she was much opened with the people's lying in her,[9] which kept us long there, for it was sixteen or seventeen days before the carpenter had finished her. Our people went on shore to refresh themselves, and our women to wash, as they had great need. But whilst we lay thus still, hoping our shallop would be ready in five or six days at the furthest, but our carpenter made slow work of it, so that some of our people, impatient of delay, desired for our better furtherance to travel by land into the country, which was not without appearance of danger, not having the shallop with them, nor means to carry provision, but on their backs, to see whether it might be fit for us to seat in or no, and the rather because as we sailed into the harbor there seemed to be a river opening itself into the main land. The willingness of the persons was liked, but the thing itself, in regard of the danger, was rather permitted than approved, and so with cautions, directions, and instructions, sixteen men were set out with every man his musket, sword, and corslet, under the conduct of Captain Miles Standish, unto whom was adjoined, for counsel and advice, William Bradford, Stephen Hopkins, and Edward Tilley.

Wednesday, the 15th of November, they were set ashore, and when they had ordered themselves in the order of a

8 A large longboat which can be rowed, or fitted with a small mast and sails.
9 An indication of the overcrowded conditions aboard the *Mayflower* is the fact that some passengers slept in the shallop, which had been partially disassembled for easier storage.

single file and marched about the space of a mile, by the sea they espied five or six people with a dog, coming towards them, who were savages, who when they saw them, ran into the wood and whistled the dog after them, etc. First they supposed them to be Master Jones, the master, and some of his men, for they were ashore and knew of their coming, but after they knew them to be Indians they marched after them into the woods, lest other of the Indians should lie in ambush. But when the Indians saw our men following them, they ran away with might and main and our men turned out of the wood after them, for it was the way they intended to go, but they could not come near them. They followed them that night about ten miles by the trace of their footings, and saw how they had come the same way they went, and at a turning perceived how they ran up a hill, to see whether they followed them. At length night came upon them, and they were constrained to take up their lodging, so they set forth three sentinels, and the rest, some kindled a fire, and others fetched wood, and there held our rendezvous that night.

In the morning so soon as we could see the trace, we proceeded on our journey, and had the track until we had compassed the head of a long creek, and there they took into another wood, and we after them, supposing to find some of their dwellings, but we marched through boughs and bushes, and under hills and valleys, which tore our very armor in pieces, and yet could meet with none of them, nor their houses, nor find any fresh water, which we greatly desired, and stood in need of, for we brought neither beer nor water with us, and our victuals was only biscuit and Holland cheese, and a little bottle of aquavitae, so as we were sore athirst. About ten o'clock we came into a deep valley, full of brush, wood-gaile, and long grass, through which we found little paths or tracks, and there we saw a deer, and found springs of fresh water, of which we were heartily glad, and sat us down and drunk our first

New England water with as much delight as ever we drunk drink in all our lives.

When we had refreshed ourselves, we directed our course full south, that we might come to the shore, which within a short while after we did, and there made a fire, that they in the ship might see where we were (as we had direction) and so marched on towards this supposed river. And as we went in another valley we found a fine clear pond of fresh water, being about a musket shot broad and twice as long. There grew also many fine vines, and fowl and deer haunted there; there grew much sassafras.[10] From thence we went on, and found much plain ground, about fifty acres, fit for the plow, and some signs where the Indians had formerly planted their corn. After this, some thought it best, for nearness of the river, to go down and travel on the sea sands, by which means some of our men were tired, and lagged behind. So we stayed and gathered them up, and struck into the land again, where we found a little path to certain heaps of sand, one whereof was covered with old mats, and had a wooden thing like a mortar whelmed[11] on the top of it, and an earthen pot laid in a little hole at the end thereof. We, musing what it might be, digged and found a bow, and, as we thought, arrows, but they were rotten. We supposed there were many other things, but because we deemed them graves, we put in the bow again and made it up as it was, and left the rest untouched, because we thought it would be odious unto them to ransack their sepulchres.

We went on further and found new stubble, of which they had gotten corn this year, and many walnut trees full of nuts, and great store of strawberries, and some vines. Passing thus a field or two, which were not great, we came

10 The frequent mention of sassafras is understandable in view of the immense commercial value of that plant in the early seveneenth century; the root and bark were sold as medicines throughout the Old World.

11 overturned

to another which had also been new gotten, and there we found where a house had been, and four or five old planks laid together; also we found a great kettle which had been some ship's kettle and brought out of Europe.[12] There was also a heap of sand, made like the former — but it was newly done, we might see how they had paddled it with their hands — which we digged up, and in it we found a little old basket full of fair Indian corn, and digged further and found a fine great new basket full of very fair corn of this year, with some thirty-six goodly ears of corn, some yellow, and some red, and others mixed with blue, which was a very goodly sight. The basket was round, and narrow at the top; it held about three or four bushels, which was as much as two of us could lift up from the ground, and was very handsomely and cunningly made. But whilst we were busy about these things, we set our men sentinel in a round ring, all but two or three which digged up the corn. We were in suspense what to do with it and the kettle, and at length, after much consultation, we concluded to take the kettle and as much of the corn as we could carry away with us; and when our shallop came, if we could find any of the people, and come to parley with them, we would give them the kettle again, and satisfy them for their corn.[13] So we took all the ears, and put a good deal of the loose corn in the kettle for two men to bring away on a staff; besides, they that could put any into their pockets filled the same. The rest we buried again, for we were so laden with armor that we could carry no more.

Not far from this place we found the remainder of an old fort, or palisade, which as we conceived had been made by some Christians. This was also hard by that place which we thought had been a river, unto which we went and found it so to be, dividing itself into two arms by a high bank.

12 Cf. note 2, p. 16.
13 It is little wonder that the Indians later took the Pilgrims to task for having appropriated dried corn from such caches where it had been stored.

Standing right by the cut or mouth which came from the sea, that which was next unto us was the less; the other arm was more than twice as big, and not unlike to be a harbor for ships. But whether it be a fresh river, or only an indraught of the sea, we had no time to discover, for we had commandment to be out but two days. Here also we saw two canoes, the one on the one side, the other on the other side; we could not believe it was a canoe, till we came near it. So we returned, leaving the further discovery hereof to our shallop, and came that night back again to the fresh water pond, and there we made our rendezvous that night, making a great fire, and a barricade to windward of us, and kept good watch with three sentinels all night, every one standing when his turn came, while five or six inches of match was burning.[14] It proved a very rainy night.

In the morning we took our kettle and sunk it in the pond, and trimmed our muskets, for few of them would go off because of the wet, and so coasted the wood again to come home, in which we were shrewdly puzzled, and lost our way. As we wandered we came to a tree, where a young sprit[15] was bowed down over a bow, and some acorns strewed underneath. Stephen Hopkins said it had been to catch some deer. So as we were looking at it, William Bradford being in the rear, when he came looked also upon it, and as he went about, it gave a sudden jerk up, and he was immediately caught by the leg. It was a very pretty device, made with a rope of their own making and having a noose as artificially[16] made as any roper in England can make, and as like ours as can be, which we brought away with us. In the end we got out of the wood, and were fallen about a mile too high above the creek, where we saw three bucks, but we had rather have had one of them.[17] We

14 Most of their guns were matchlocks.
15 sapling
16 artfully; skillfully
17 A quaint touch of humor.

also did spring three couple of partridges, and as we came along by the creek we saw great flocks of wild geese and ducks, but they were very fearful of us. So we marched some while in the woods, some while on the sands, and other while in the water up to the knees, till at length we came near the ship, and then we shot off our pieces, and the long boat came to fetch us. Master Jones and Master Carver being on the shore, with many of our people, came to meet us. And thus we came both weary and welcome home, and delivered in our corn into the store, to be kept for seed, for we knew not how to come by any, and therefore were very glad, purposing, so soon as we could meet with any of the inhabitants of that place, to make them large satisfaction. This was our first discovery, whilst our shallop was in repairing.

Our people did make things as fitting as they could, and time would, in seeking out wood, and helving[18] of tools, and sawing of timber to build a new shallop. But the discommodiousness of the harbor did much hinder us for we could neither go to nor come from the shore, but at high water, which was much to our hindrance and hurt, for oftentimes they waded to the middle of the thigh, and oft to the knees, to go and come from land. Some did it necessarily, and some for their own pleasure, but it brought to the most, if not to all, coughs and colds, the weather proving suddenly cold and stormy, which afterwards turned to the scurvy,[19] whereof many died.

When our shallop was fit — indeed, before she was fully fitted, for there was two days' work after bestowed on her — there was appointed some twenty-four men of our own, and armed, then to go and make a more full discovery of the rivers before mentioned. Master Jones was desirous to go with us, and we took such of his sailors as he thought useful for us, so as we were in all about thirty-four men.

18 hafting
19 More likely, pneumonia.

We made Master Jones our leader, for we thought it best herein to gratify his kindness and forwardness. When we were set forth, it proved rough weather and cross winds, so as we were constrained, some in the shallop, and others in the long boat, to row to the nearest shore the wind would suffer them to go unto, and then to wade out above the knees. The wind was so strong as the shallop could not keep the water, but was forced to harbor there that night, but we marched six or seven miles further, and appointed the shallop to come to us as soon as they could. It blowed and did snow all that day and night, and froze withal; some of our people that are dead took the original of their death here.

The next day, about eleven o'clock, our shallop came to us and we shipped ourselves, and the wind being good, we sailed to the river we formerly discovered, which we named Cold Harbor, to which when we came we found it not navigable for ships, yet we thought it might be a good harbor for boats, for it flows there twelve foot at high water. We landed our men between the two creeks and marched some four or five miles by the greater of them, and the shallop followed us. At length night grew on, and our men were tired with marching up and down the steep hills and deep valleys which lay half a foot thick with snow. Master Jones, wearied with marching, was desirous we should take up our lodging, though some of us would have marched further, so we made there our rendezvous for that night, under a few pine trees. And as it fell out, we got three fat geese and six ducks to our supper, which we ate with soldiers' stomachs, for we had eaten little all that day. Our resolution was next morning to go up to the head of this river, for we supposed it would prove fresh water, but in the morning our resolution held not, because many liked not the hilliness of the soil, and badness of the harbor. So we turned towards the other creek, that we might go over and look for the rest of the corn that we left behind when we were here before.

When we came to the creek we saw the canoe lie on the dry ground, and a flock of geese in the river, at which one made a shot and killed a couple of them, and we launched the canoe and fetched them and when we had done, she carried us over by seven or eight at once. This done, we marched to the place where we had the corn formerly, which place we called Cornhill, and digged and found the rest, of which we were very glad. We also digged in a place a little further off, and found a bottle of oil. We went to another place which we had seen before, and digged, and found more corn, viz. two or three baskets full of Indian wheat,[20] and a bag of beans, with a good many of fair wheat[20] ears. Whilst some of us were digging up this, some others found another heap of corn, which they digged up also, so as we had in all about ten bushels, which will serve us sufficiently for seed. And sure it was God's good providence that we found this corn, for else we know not how we should have done, for we knew not how we should find or meet with any Indians, except it be to do us a mischief.[21] Also, we had never in all likelihood seen a grain of it if we had not made our first journey, for the ground was now covered with snow, and so hard frozen that we were fain with our cutlasses and short swords to hew and carve the ground a foot deep, and then wrest it up with levers, for we had forgot to bring other tools. Whilst we were in this employment, foul weather being towards, Master Jones was earnest to go aboard, but sundry of us desired to make further discovery and to find out the Indians' habitations. So we sent home with him our weakest people, and some that were sick, and all the corn, and eighteen of us stayed still, and lodged there that night, and desired that the shal-

Note.

20 I.e., corn.
21 Knowledge of Indian attacks on white settlers in the Spanish colonies and in what is now Virginia had led the Pilgrims to expect ill of them.

lop might return to us next day and bring us some mattocks and spades with them.

The next morning we followed certain beaten paths and tracks of the Indians into the woods, supposing they would have led us into some town, or houses. After we had gone a while, we light upon a very broad beaten path, well nigh two feet broad. Then we lighted all our matches[22] and prepared ourselves, concluding that we were near their dwellings, but in the end we found it to be only a path made to drive deer in, when the Indians hunt, as we supposed.

When we had marched five or six miles into the woods and could find no signs of any people, we returned again another way, and as we came into the plain ground we found a place like a grave, but it was much bigger and longer than any we had yet seen. It was also covered with boards, so as we mused what it should be, and resolved to dig it up, where we found, first a mat, and under that a fair bow, and there another mat, and under that a board about three quarters[23] long, finely carved and painted, with three tines, or broaches, on the top, like a crown. Also between the mats we found bowls, trays, dishes, and such like trinkets. At length we came to a fair new mat, and under that two bundles, the one bigger, the other less. We opened the greater and found in it a great quantity of fine and perfect red powder, and in it the bones and skull of a man. The skull had fine yellow hair still on it, and some of the flesh unconsumed; there was bound up with it a knife, a packneedle,[24] and two or three old iron things. It was bound up in a sailor's canvas cassock, and a pair of cloth breeches. The red powder was a kind of embalment, and yielded a strong, but no offensive smell; it was as fine as any flour. We opened the less bundle likewise, and found

22 I.e., the slow-burning wicks of their matchlock muskets.
23 [of a yard]
24 a large strong needle used for sewing packages in stout cloth

of the same powder in it, and the bones and head of a little child. About the legs and other parts of it was bound strings and bracelets of fine white beads; there was also by it a little bow, about three quarters long, and some other odd knacks. We brought sundry of the prettiest things away with us, and covered the corpse up again. After this, we digged in sundry like places, but found no more corn, nor any thing else but graves.

There was variety of opinions amongst us about the embalmed person. Some thought it was an Indian lord and king. Others said the Indians have all black hair, and never any was seen with brown or yellow hair. Some thought it was a Christian of some special note, which had died amongst them, and they thus buried him to honor him. Others thought they had killed him, and did it in triumph over him.

Whilst we were thus ranging and searching, two of the sailors, which were newly come on the shore, by chance espied two houses which had been lately dwelt in, but the people were gone. They, having their pieces and hearing nobody, entered the houses and took out some things, and durst not stay but came again and told us. So some seven or eight of us went with them, and found how we had gone within a flight shot of them before. The houses were made with long young sapling trees, bended and both ends stuck into the ground. They were made round, like unto an arbor, and covered down to the ground with thick and well wrought mats, and the door was not over a yard high, made of a mat to open. The chimney was a wide open hole in the top, for which they had a mat to cover it close when they pleased. One might stand and go upright in them. In the midst of them were four little trunches[25] knocked into the ground, and small sticks laid over, on which they hung their pots, and what they had to seethe.[26]

25 stakes
26 simmer; boil

Round about the fire they lay on mats, which are their beds. The houses were double matted, for as they were matted without, so were they within, with newer and fairer mats. In the houses we found wooden bowls, trays and dishes, earthen pots, handbaskets made of crabshells wrought together, also an English pail or bucket; it wanted a bail, but it had two iron ears. There was also baskets of sundry sorts, bigger and some lesser, finer and some coarser; some were curiously wrought with black and white in pretty works, and sundry other of their household stuff. We found also two or three deer's heads, one whereof had been newly killed, for it was still fresh. There was also a company of deer's feet stuck up in the houses, harts' horns, and eagles' claws, and sundry such like things there was, also two or three baskets full of parched acorns, pieces of fish, and a piece of a broiled herring. We found also a little silk grass, and a little tobacco seed, with some other seeds which we knew not. Without was sundy bundles of flags, and sedge, bulrushes, and other stuff to make mats. There was thrust into a hollow tree two or three pieces of venison, but we thought it fitter for the dogs than for us. Some of the best things we took away with us, and left the houses standing still as they were.

So it growing towards night, and the tide almost spent, we hasted with our things down to the shallop, and got aboard that night, intending to have brought some beads and other things to have left in the houses, in sign of peace and that we meant to truck with them, but it was not done, by means of our hasty coming away from Cape Cod. But so soon as we can meet conveniently with them, we will give them full satisfaction. Thus much of our second discovery.

Having thus discovered this place, it was controversial amongst us what to do touching our abode and settling there; some thought it best, for many reasons, to abide there. As first, that there was a convenient harbor for boats, though not for ships. Secondly, good corn-ground ready to our hands, as we saw by experience in the goodly corn it yielded, which would again agree with the ground, and be natural seed for the same. Thirdly, Cape Cod was like to be a place of good fishing, for we saw daily great whales of the best kind for oil and bone, come close aboard our ship, and in fair weather swim and play about us. There was once one, when the sun shone warm, came and lay above water as if she had been dead, for a good while together, within half a musket shot of the ship, at which two were prepared to shoot to see whether she would stir or no. He that gave fire first, his musket flew in pieces, both stock and barrel, yet, thanks be to God, neither he nor any man else was hurt with it, though many were there about. But when the whale saw her time, she gave a snuff, and away. Fourthly, the place was likely to be healthful, secure, and defensible.

But the last and especial reason was, that now the heart of winter and unseasonable weather was come upon us, so that we could not go upon coasting and discovery without danger of losing men and boat, upon which would follow the overthrow of all, especially considering what variable winds and sudden storms do there arise. Also, cold and wet lodging had so tainted our people, for scarce any of us were free from vehement coughs, as if they should continue long in that estate it would endanger the lives of many, and breed diseases and infection amongst us. Again, we had yet some beer, butter, flesh, and other such victuals left, which would quickly be all gone, and then we should have nothing to comfort us in the great labor and toil we were like to undergo at the first. It was also conceived, whilst we had competent victuals, that the ship would stay with us, but when that grew low, they would be gone and let us shift as we could.

Others again, urged greatly the going to Anguum, or Angoum,[27] a place twenty leagues off to the northwards,

27 Agawam; now, Ipswich, Massachusetts.

which they had heard to be an excellent harbor for ships, better ground, and better fishing. Secondly, for anything we knew, there might be hard by us a far better seat, and it should be a great hindrance to seat where we should remove again. Thirdly, the water was but in ponds, and it was thought there would be none in summer, or very little. Fourthly, the water there must be fetched up a steep hill. But to omit many reasons and replies used hereabouts, it was in the end concluded to make some discovery within the bay, but in no case so far as Anguum. Besides, Robert Coppin, our pilot, made relation of a great navigable river and good harbor in the other headland of this bay, almost right over against Cape Cod, being in a right line not much above eight leagues distant, in which he had been once; and because that one of the wild men with whom they had some trucking stole a harping iron[28] from them, they called it Thievish Harbor. And beyond that place they were enjoined not to go, whereupon, a company was chosen to go out upon a third discovery. Whilst some were employed in this discovery, it pleased God that Mistress White was brought a-bed of a son, which was called Peregrine.

The 5th day, we, through God's mercy, escaped a great danger by the foolishness of a boy, one of Francis Billington's sons, who, in his father's absence, had got gunpowder and had shot of a piece or two, and made squibs, and there being a fowling-piece charged in his father's cabin, shot her off in the cabin; there being a little barrel of powder half full, scattered in and about the cabin, the fire being within four feet of the bed between the decks, and many flints and iron things about the cabin, and many people about the fire, and yet, by God's mercy, no harm done.

Wednesday, the 6th of December, it was resolved our discoverers should set forth, for the day before was too foul weather, and so they did, though it was well o'er the day

28 harpoon

ere all things could be ready. So ten of our men were appointed who were of themselves willing to undertake it, to wit, Captain Standish, Master Carver, William Bradford, Edward Winslow, John Tilley, Edward Tilley, John Howland, and three of London, Richard Warren, Stephen Hopkins, and Edward Dotte, and two of our seamen, John Allerton and Thomas English. Of the ship's company there went two of the master's mates, Master Clarke and Master Coppin, the master gunner, and three sailors. The narration of which discovery follows, penned by one of the company.

Wednesday, the 6th of December, we set out, being very cold and hard weather. We were a long while after we launched from the ship before we could get clear of a sandy point which lay within less than a furlong of the same. In which time two were very sick, and Edward Tilley had like to have sounded[29] with cold; the gunner also was sick unto death, (but hope of trucking made him to go), and so remained all that day and the next night. At length we got clear of the sandy point and got up our sails, and within an hour or two we got under the weather shore, and then had smoother water and better sailing, but it was very cold, for the water froze on our clothes and made them many times like coats of iron. We sailed six or seven leagues by the shore, but saw neither river nor creek; at length we met with a tongue of land, being flat off from the shore, with a sandy point. We bore up to gain the point, and found there a fair income or road of a bay, being a league over at the narrowest, and some two or three in length, but we made right over to the land before us, and left the discovery of this income till the next day. As we drew near to the shore, we espied some ten or twelve Indians very busy about a black thing — what it was we could not tell — till afterwards they saw us, and ran to and fro as if they had been carrying something away. We landed a league or

29 swooned

two from them, and had much ado to put ashore anywhere, it lay so full of flat sands. When we came to shore, we made us a barricade, and got firewood, and set out our sentinels, and betook us to our lodging, such as it was. We saw the smoke of the fire which the savages made that night, about four or five miles from us.

In the morning we divided our company, some eight in the shallop, and the rest on the shore went to discover this place, but we found it only to be a bay, without either river or creek coming into it. Yet we deemed it to be as good a harbor as Cape Cod, for they that sounded it found a ship might ride in five fathom water. We on the land found it to be a level soil, though none of the fruitfullest. We saw two becks[30] of fresh water, which were the first running streams that we saw in the country, but one might stride over them. We found also a great fish, called a grampus, dead on the sands; they in the shallop found two of them also in the bottom of the bay, dead in like sort. They were cast up at high water, and could not get off for the frost and ice. They were some five or six paces long, and about two inches thick of fat, and fleshed like a swine; they would have yielded a great deal of oil if there had been time and means to have taken it. So we finding nothing for our turn, both we and our shallop returned.

We then directed our course along the sea sands, to the place where we first saw the Indians. When we were there, we saw it was also a grampus which they were cutting up; they cut it into long rands or pieces, about an ell[31] long, and two handfull broad. We found here and there a piece scattered by the way, as it seemed, for haste. This place the most were minded we should call the Grampus Bay, because we found so many of them there. We followed the track of the Indians' bare feet a good way on the sands; at length we saw where they struck into the woods

30 brooks
31 I.e., 45 inches.

by the side of a pond. As we went to view the place, one said he thought he saw an Indian house among the trees, so went up to see. And here we and the shallop lost sight one of another till night, it being now about nine or ten o'clock.

So we light on a path, but saw no house, and followed a great way into the woods. At length we found where corn had been set, but not that year. Anon we found a great burying place, one part whereof was encompassed with a large palisade, like a churchyard, with young spires[32] four or five yards long, set as close one by another as they could, two or three feet in the ground. Within it was full of graves, some bigger and some less; some were also paled about, and others had like an Indian house made over them, but not matted. Those graves were more sumptuous than those at Cornhill, yet we digged none of them up, but only viewed them, and went our way. Without the palisade were graves also, but not so costly. From this place we went and found more corn-ground, but not of this year. As we ranged we light on four or five Indian houses, which had been lately dwelt in, but they were uncovered, and had no mats about them, else they were like those we found at Cornhill but had not been so lately dwelt in. There was nothing left but two or three pieces of old mats, and a little sedge. Also, a little further we found two baskets full of parched acorns hid in the ground, which we supposed had been corn when we began to dig the same; we cast earth thereon again and went our way. All this while we saw no people.

We went ranging up and down till the sun began to draw low, and then we hasted out of the woods, that we might come to our shallop, which when we were out of the woods, we espied a great way off, and called them to come unto us, the which they did as soon as they could, for it was not yet high water. They were exceeding glad to

32 saplings

see us (for they feared because they had not seen us in so long a time), thinking we would have kept by the shore side. So being both weary and faint, for we had eaten nothing all that day, we fell to make our rendezvous and get firewood, which always costs us a great deal of labor. By that time we had done, and our shallop come to us, it was within night, and we fed upon such victuals as we had, and betook us to our rest, after we had set out our watch. About midnight we heard a great and hideous cry, and our sentinels called, "Arm! Arm!" So we bestirred ourselves and shot off a couple of muskets, and the noise ceased; we concluded that it was a company of wolves or foxes, for one told us he had heard such a noise in Newfoundland.

About five o'clock in the morning we began to be stirring, and two or three which doubted whether their pieces would go off or no made trial of them, and shot them off, but thought nothing at all. After prayer we prepared ourselves for breakfast and for a journey, and it being now the twilight in the morning, it was thought meet to carry the things down to the shallop. Some said it was not best to carry the armor down; others said they would be readier; two or three said they would not carry theirs till they went themselves, but mistrusting nothing at all. As it fell out, the water not being high enough, they laid the things down upon the shore and came up to breakfast. Anon, all upon a sudden, we heard a great and strange cry, which we knew to be the same voices, though they varied their notes. One of our company, being abroad, came running in and cried, "They are men! Indians! Indians!" and withal, their arrows came flying amongst us. Our men ran out with all speed to recover their arms, as by the good providence of God they did. In the meantime, Captain Miles Standish, having a snaphance[33] ready, made a shot, and after him another. After they two had shot, other two of us were ready, but he wished us not to shoot till we could take aim,

Our first combat with the *Indians*.

33 A kind of flintlock musket.

35

for we knew not what need we should have, and there were four only of us which had their arms there ready, and stood before the open side of our barricade, which was first assaulted. They thought it best to defend it, lest the enemy should take it and our stuff, and so have the more vantage against us. Our care was no less for the shallop, but we hoped all the rest would defend it; we called unto them to know how it was with them, and they answered, "Well! Well!" every one and, "Be of good courage!" We heard three of their pieces go off, and the rest called for a firebrand to light their matches. One took a log out of the fire on his shoulder and went and carried it unto them, which was thought did not a little discourage our enemies. The cry of our enemies was dreadful, especially when our men ran out to recover their arms; their note was after this manner, *"Woach woach ha ha hach woach."*[34] Our men were no sooner come to their arms, but the enemy was ready to assault them.

There was a lusty man and no whit less valiant, who was thought to be their captain, stood behind a tree within half a musket shot of us, and there let his arrows fly at us. He was seen to shoot three arrows, which were all avoided, for he at whom the first arrow was aimed, saw it, and stooped down and it flew over him; the rest were avoided also. He stood three shots of a musket. At length one took, as he said, full aim at him, after which he gave an extraordinary cry and away they went all. We followed them about a quarter of a mile, but we left six to keep our shallop, for we were careful of our business. Then we shouted all together two several times, and shot off a couple of muskets and so returned; this we did that they might see we were not afraid of them nor discouraged.

---

34 This defies translation. It is probably less an accurate transcription of specific Algonquian words than an Englishman's vague approximation of the incomprehensible sounds which seemed threatening to him in such a context.

Thus it pleased God to vanquish our enemies and give us deliverance. By their noise we could not guess that they were less than thirty or forty, though some thought that they were many more. Yet in the dark of the morning we could not so well discern them among the trees, as they could see us by our fireside. We took up eighteen of their arrows which we have sent to England by Master Jones, some whereof were headed with brass, others with harts' horn, and others with eagles' claws. Many more no doubt were shot, for these we found were almost covered with leaves; yet, by the especial providence of God, none of them either hit or hurt us though many came close by us and on every side of us, and some coats which hung up in our baricade were shot through and through.

So after we had given God thanks for our deliverance, we took our shallop and went on our journey, and called this place, The First Encounter. From thence we intended to have sailed to the aforesaid Thievish Harbor, if we found no convenient harbor by the way. Having the wind good, we sailed all that day along the coast about fifteen leagues, but saw neither river nor creek to put into. After we had sailed an hour or two, it began to snow and rain, and to be bad weather. About the midst of the afternoon, the wind increased and the seas began to be very rough, and the hinges of the rudder broke so that we could steer no longer with it, but two men with much ado were fain to serve with a couple of oars. The seas were grown so great that we were much troubled and in great danger, and night grew on. Anon Master Coppin bade us be of good cheer; he saw the harbor. As we drew near, the gale being stiff and we bearing great sail to get in, split our mast in three pieces, and were like to have cast away our shallop. Yet, by God's mercy, recovering ourselves, we had the flood with us, and struck into the harbor.

Now he that thought that had been the place was deceived, it being a place where not any of us had been before, and coming into the harbor, he that was our pilot did bear up northward, which if we had continued we had been cast away. Yet still the Lord kept us, and we bore up for an island before us, and recovering of that island, being compassed about with many rocks, and dark night growing upon us, it pleased the Divine Providence that we fell upon a place of sandy ground, where our shallop did ride safe and secure all that night, and coming upon a strange island kept our watch all night in the rain upon that island. And in the morning we marched about it and found no inhabitants at all, and here we made our rendezvous all that day, being Saturday, 10th of December. On the Sabbath day we rested, and on Monday we sounded the harbor, and found it a very good harbor for our shipping. We marched also into the land, and found divers cornfields, and little running brooks, a place very good for situation, so we returned to our ship again with good news to the rest of our people, which did much comfort their hearts.[35]

On the 15th day we weighed anchor, to go to the place we had discovered, and coming within two leagues of the land, we could not fetch the harbor, but were fain to put room again towards Cape Cod, our course lying west, and the wind was at northwest. But it pleased God that the next day, being Saturday the 16th day, the wind came fair and we put to sea again, and came safely into a safe harbor; and within half an hour the wind changed, so as if we had been letted[36] but a little, we had gone back to Cape Cod.

This harbor is a bay greater than Cape Cod, compassed with a goodly land, and in the bay, two fine islands uninhabited, wherein are nothing but wood, oaks, pines, walnuts, beech, sassafras, vines, and other trees which we know

---

35 The landing at Plymouth is reported here as having been almost fortuitous, although some scholars believe that a few of the leaders may long before have planned to settle at that site. Clearly there is nothing here that can be construed as referring to "Plymouth Rock."

36 hindered

not. This bay is a most hopeful place, innumerable store of fowl, and excellent good, and cannot but be of fish in their seasons; skote,[37] cod, turbot, and herring, we have tasted of, abundance of mussels the greatest and best that ever we saw; crabs and lobsters, in their time infinite. It is in fashion like a sickle or fish-hook.

Monday the 18th day, we went a-land, manned with the master of the ship and three or four of the sailors. We marched along the coast in the woods some seven or eight miles, but saw not an Indian nor an Indian house; only we found where formerly had been some inhabitants, and where they had planted their corn. We found not any navigable river, but four or five small running brooks of very sweet fresh water, that all run into the sea. The land for the crust of the earth is, a spit's[38] depth, excellent black mould,[39] and fat[40] in some places, two or three great oaks but not very thick, pines, walnuts, beech, ash, birch, hazel, holly, asp,[41] sassafras in abundance, and vines everywhere, cherry trees, plum trees, and many others which we know not. Many kinds of herbs we found here in winter, as strawberry leaves innumerable, sorrel, yarrow, carvel, brooklime, liverwort, watercresses, great store of leeks and onions, and an excellent strong kind of flax and hemp. Here is sand, gravel, and excellent clay, no better in the world, excellent for pots, and will wash like soap, and great store of stone, though somewhat soft, and the best water that ever we drank, and the brooks now begin to be full of fish. That night, many being weary with marching, we went aboard again.

The next morning, being Tuesday the 19th of December, we went again to discover further; some went on land, and some in the shallop. The land we found as the former day

37 Presumably a misprint for *skate*.
38 spade's
39 loose friable earth
40 fertile; rich
41 aspen

we did, and we found a creek, and went up three English miles. A very pleasant river, at full sea a bark of thirty tons may go up, but at low water scarce our shallop could pass. This place we had a great liking to plant in, but that it was so far from our fishing, our principal profit,[42] and so encompassed with woods that we should be in much danger of the savages, and our number being so little, and so much ground to clear, so as we thought good to quit and clear that place till we were of more strength. Some of us having a good mind for safety to plant in the greater isle,[43] we crossed the bay which is there five or six miles over, and found the isle about a mile and a half or two miles about, all wooded, and no fresh water but two or three pits, that we doubted of fresh water in summer, and so full of wood as we could hardly clear so much as to serve us for corn. Besides, we judged it cold for our corn, and some part very rocky, yet divers thought of it as a place defensible, and of great security.

That night we returned again a-shipboard, with resolution the next morning to settle on some of those places; so in the morning, after we had called on God for direction, we came to this resolution: to go presently ashore again, and to take a better view of two places, which we thought most fitting for us, for we could not now take time for further search or consideration, our victuals being much spent, especially our beer, and it being now the 19th of December. After our landing and viewing of the places,

42 The Pilgrims were in a situation far different from that of later pioneers who settled elsewhere as independent farmers. According to the terms of their stringent contract with the "merchant adventurers," their primary concern was to produce salable goods (e.g., fish, lumber, furs) for their sponsors. This commitment was to endure seven years, during which the sponsors were to continue their support of the settlers. The English businessmen seem to have taken full advantage of the dependent situation of the Pilgrims who had no other sources of supply nor outlets for their goods.

43 Clark's Island, in Plymouth Harbor.

so well as we could we came to a conclusion, by most voices, to set on the mainland, on the first place, on a high ground, where there is a great deal of land cleared, and hath been planted with corn three or four years ago, and there is a very sweet brook runs under the hill side, and many delicate springs of as good water as can be drunk, and where we may harbor our shallops and boats exceeding well, and in this brook much good fish in their seasons; on the further side of the river also much corn-ground cleared. In one field is a great hill on which we point to make a platform and plant our ordnance, which will command all round about. From thence we may see into the bay, and far into the sea, and we may see thence Cape Cod. Our greatest labor will be fetching of our wood, which is half a quarter of an English mile, but there is enough so far off. What people inhabit here we yet know not, for as yet we have seen none. So there we made our rendezvous, and a place for some of our people, about twenty, resolving in the morning to come all ashore and to build houses.

But the next morning, being Thursday the 21st of December, it was stormy and wet, that we could not go ashore, and those that remained there all night could do nothing, but were wet, not having daylight enough to make them a sufficient court of guard[44] to keep them dry. All that night it blew and rained extremely; it was so tempestuous that the shallop could not go on land so soon as was meet, for they had no victuals on land. About eleven o'clock the shallop went off with much ado with provision, but could not return; it blew so strong and was such foul weather that we were forced to let fall our anchor and ride with three anchors ahead.

Friday, the 22nd, the storm still continued, that we could not get a-land nor they come to us aboard. This morning good-wife[45] Allerton was delivered of a son, but dead born.

---

44 guard-house; i.e., a shelter affording some security against possible attack
45 mistress of a household, (a title of respect)

Saturday, the 23rd, so many of us as could, went on shore, felled and carried timber, to provide themselves stuff for building.

Sunday, the 24th, our people on shore heard a cry of some savages (as they thought) which caused an alarm, and to stand on their guard, expecting an assault, but all was quiet.

Monday, the 25th day, we went on shore. some to fell timber, some to saw, some to rive, and some to carry, so no man rested all that day. But towards night some, as they were at work, heard a noise of some Indians, which caused us all to go to our muskets, but we heard no further. So we came aboard again, and left some twenty to keep the court of guard. That night we had a sore storm of wind and rain.

Monday, the 25th day, we went on shore, some to fell drink water aboard, but at night the master caused us to have some beer, and so on board we had divers times now and then some beer, but on shore none at all.

Tuesday, the 26th, it was foul weather, that we could not go ashore.

Wednesday, the 27th, we went to work again.

Thursday, the 28th of December, so many as could went to work on the hill where we purposed to build our platform for our ordnance, and which doth command all the plain and the bay, and from whence we may see far into the sea, and might be easier impaled, having two rows of houses and a fair street. So in the afternoon we went to measure out the grounds, and first we took notice how many families there were, willing all single men that had no wives to join with some family, as they thought fit, that so we might build fewer houses, which was done, and we reduced them to nineteen families. To greater families we allotted larger plots, to every person half a pole in breadth, and three in length,[46] and so lots were cast where every man should lie, which was done, and staked out. We

46 I.e., 8¼ by 49½ feet.

thought this proportion was large enough at the first for houses and gardens, to impale them round, considering the weakness of our people, many of them growing ill with cold, for our former discoveries in frost and storms, and the wading at Cape Cod had brought much weakness amongst us, which increased so every day more and more, and after was the cause of many of their deaths.

Friday and Saturday, we fitted ourselves for our labor, but our people on shore were much troubled and discouraged with rain and wet, that day being very stormy and cold. We saw great smokes of fire made by the Indians, about six or seven miles from us, as we conjectured.

Monday, the 1st of January, we went betimes to work. We were much hindered in lying so far off from the land, and fain to go as the tide served, that we lost much time, for our ship drew so much water[47] that she lay a mile and almost a half off, though a ship of seventy or eighty tons at high water may come to the shore.

Wednesday, the 3rd of January, some of our people being abroad to get and gather thatch, they saw great fires of the Indians, and were at their corn-fields, yet saw none of the savages, nor had seen any of them since we came to this bay.

Thursday, the 4th of January, Captain Miles Standish with four or five more, went to see if they could meet with any of the savages in that place where the fires were made. They went to some of their houses, but not lately inhabited, yet could they not meet with any. As they came home, they shot at an eagle and killed her, which was excellent meat; it was hardly to be discerned from mutton.

Friday, the 5th of January, one of the sailors found alive upon the shore a herring, which the master had to his supper, which put us in hope of fish, but as yet we had got but one cod; we wanted small hooks.

Saturday, the 6th of January, Master Martin was very

47 The *Mayflower* was a vessel of 180 tons.

sick, and to our judgment no hope of life, so Master Carver was sent for to come aboard to speak with him about his accounts, who came the next morning.

Monday, the 8th day of January, was a very fair day, and we went betimes to work. Master Jones sent the shallop, as he had formerly done, to see where fish could be got. They had a great storm at sea, and were in some danger; at night they returned with three great seals and an excellent good cod, which did assure us that we should have plenty of fish shortly.

This day, Francis Billington, having the week before seen from the top of a tree on a high hill a great sea as he thought, went with one of the master's mates to see it. They went three miles and then came to a great water, divided into two great lakes, the bigger of them five or six miles in circuit, and in it an isle of a cable length[48] square, the other three miles in compass; in their estimation they are fine fresh water, full of fish, and fowl. A brook issues from it; it will be an excellent help for us in time. They found seven or eight Indian houses, but not lately inhabited. When they saw the houses they were in some fear, for they were but two persons and one piece.

Tuesday, the 9th of January, was a reasonable fair day, and we went to labor that day in the building of our town, in two rows of houses for more safety. We divided by lot the plot of ground whereon to build our town. After the proportion formerly alloted, we agreed that every man should build his own house, thinking by that course men would make more haste than working in common. The common house, in which for the first we made our rendezvous, being near finished wanted only covering, it being about twenty feet square. Some should make mortar, and some gather thatch, so that in four days half of it was thatched. Frost and foul weather hindered us much, this time of the year seldom could we work half the week.

48 I.e., approximately 600 feet.

Thursday, the 11th, William Bradford being at work (for it was a fair day) was vehemently taken with a grief and pain, and so shot to his huckle-bone.[49] It was doubted that he would have instantly died; he got cold in the former discoveries, especially the last, and felt some pain in his ankles by times, but he grew a little better towards night and in time, through God's mercy in the use of means, recovered.

Friday, the 12th, we went to work, but about noon it began to rain that it forced us to give over work.

This day two of our people put us in great sorrow and care; there was four sent to gather and cut thatch in the morning, and two of them, John Goodman and Peter Brown, having cut thatch all the forenoon, went to a further place, and willed the other two to bind up that which was cut and to follow them. So they did, being about a mile and a half from our plantation. But when the two came after, they could not find them, nor hear any thing of them at all, though they hallooed and shouted as loud as they could, so they returned to the company and told them of it. Whereupon Master Leaver[50] and three or four more went to seek them, but could hear nothing of them, so they returning, sent more, but that night they could hear nothing at all of them. The next day they armed ten or twelve men out, verily thinking the Indians had surprised them. They went seeking seven or eight miles, but could neither see nor hear any thing at all, so they returned, with much discomfort to us all.

These two that were missed, at dinner time took their meat in their hands, and would go walk and refresh themselves. So going a little off they find a lake of water, and having a great mastiff bitch with them and a spaniel, by the water side they found a great deer; the dogs chased

49 hip-bone
50 Presumably a misprint for *Carver*. There is no other mention of a Leaver in the party.

him, and they followed so far as they lost themselves and could not find the way back. They wandered all that afternoon being wet, and at night it did freeze and snow. They were slenderly apparelled and had no weapons but each one his sickle, nor any victuals. They ranged up and down and could find none of the savages' habitations. When it drew to night they were much perplexed, for they could find neither harbor nor meat, but, in frost and snow were forced to make the earth their bed and the element their covering. And another thing did very much terrify them; they heard, as they thought, two lions roaring exceedingly for a long time together, and a third, that they thought was very near them. So not knowing what to do, they resolved to climb up into a tree as their safest refuge, though that would prove an intolerable cold lodging; so they stood at the tree's root, that when the lions came they might take their opportunity of climbing up. The bitch they were fain to hold by the neck, for she would have been gone to the lion; but it pleased God so to dispose, that the wild beasts came not. So they walked up and down under the tree all night; it was an extreme cold night. So soon as it was light they travelled again, passing by many lakes and brooks and woods, and in one place where the savages had burnt the space of five miles in length, which is a fine champaign[51] country, and even. In the afternoon, it pleased God, from a high hill they discovered the two isles in the bay, and so that night got to the plantation, being ready to faint with travail and want of victuals, and almost famished with cold. John Goodman was fain to have his shoes cut off his feet they were so swelled with cold, and it was a long while after ere he was able to go; those on the shore were much comforted at their return, but they on shipboard were grieved at deeming them lost.

But the next day, being the 14th of January, in the morning about six of the clock the wind being very great, they

51 open

on shipboard spied their great new rendezvous on fire, which was to them a new discomfort, fearing because of the supposed loss of the men, that the savages had fired them. Neither could they presently go to them, for want of water, but after three quarters of an hour they went, as they had purposed the day before to keep the Sabbath on shore, because now there was the greater number of people. At their landing they heard good tidings of the return of the two men, and that the house was fired occasionally by a spark that flew into the thatch, which instantly burnt it all up but the roof stood and little hurt. The most loss was Master Carver's and William Bradford's, who then lay sick in bed, and if they had not risen with good speed, had been blown up with powder, but, through God's mercy, they had no harm. The house was as full of beds as they could lie one by another, and their muskets charged, but, blessed be God, there was no harm done.

Monday, the 15th day, it rained much all day, that they on shipboard could not go on shore, nor they on shore do any labor but were all wet.

Tuesday, Wednesday, Thursday, were very fair sunshiny days, as if it had been in April, and our people, so many as were in health, wrought cheerfully.

The 19th day we resolved to make a shed to put our common provision in, of which some were already set on shore, but at noon it rained, that we could not work. This day in the evening, John Goodman went abroad to use his lame feet, that were pitifully ill with the cold he had got, having a little spaniel with him. A little way from the plantation two great wolves ran after the dog; the dog ran to him and betwixt his legs for succor. He had nothing in his hand but took up a stick, and threw at one of them and hit him, and they presently ran both away, but came again; he got a pale-board[52] in his hand, and they sat both on their tails, grinning at him a good while, and went

52 fence-stave

their way and left him.

Saturday, 20th, we made up our shed for our common goods.

Sunday, the 21st, we kept our meeting on land.

Monday, the 22nd, was a fair day. We wrought on our houses, and in the afternoon carried up our hogsheads of meal to our common storehouse. The rest of the week we followed our business likewise.

Monday, the 29th, in the morning cold frost and sleet, but after reasonable fair; both the long-boat and the shallop brought our common goods on shore.

Tuesday and Wednesday, 30th and 31st of January, cold frosty weather and sleet, that we could not work. In the morning the master and others saw two savages that had been on the island near our ship. What they came for we could not tell; they were going so far back again before they were descried, that we could not speak with them.

Sunday, the 4th of February, was very wet and rainy, with the greatest gusts of wind that ever we had since we came forth, that though we rid in a very good harbor, yet we were in danger, because our ship was light, the goods taken out, and she unballasted; and it caused much daubing[53] of our houses to fall down.

Friday, the 9th, still the cold weather continued, that we could do little work. That afternoon our little house for our sick people was set on fire by a spark that kindled in the roof, but no great harm was done. That evening, the master going ashore, killed five geese, which he friendly distributed among the sick people. He found also a good deer killed; the savages had cut off the horns, and a wolf

---

53 This may refer to mud used for plastering the inner side of clapboard walls, typical of the frame houses which were among the first permanent buildings at Plymouth. During these early months, however, it may conceivably refer to a more fundamental structural feature in temporary huts of wattle-and-daub construction, where mud is the principal material, daubed over a framework of small saplings.

was eating of him; how he came there we could not conceive.

Friday, the 16th, was a fair day, but the northerly wind continued, which continued the frost. This day after noon one of our people being a-fowling, and having taken a stand by a creek-side in the reeds, about a mile and a half from our plantation, there came by him twelve Indians marching towards our plantation, and in the woods he heard the noise of many more. He lay close till they were passed, and then with what speed he could he went home and gave the alarm, so the people abroad in the woods returned and armed themselves, but saw none of them; only toward the evening they made a great fire, about the place where they were first discovered. Captain Miles Standish and Francis Cook, being at work in the woods, coming home, left their tools behind them, but before they returned their tools were taken away by the savages. This coming of the savages gave us occasion to keep more strict watch, and to make our pieces and furniture ready, which by the moisture and rain were out of temper.

Saturday, the 17th day, in the morning we called a meeting for the establishing of military orders among ourselves, and we chose Miles Standish our captain, and gave him authority of command in affairs. And as we were in consulation hereabouts, two savages presented themselves upon the top of a hill, over against our plantation, about a quarter of a mile and less, and made signs unto us to come unto them; we likewise made signs unto them to come to us, whereupon we armed ourselves, and stood ready, and sent two over the brook towards them, to wit, Captain Standish and Stephen Hopkins, who went towards them. Only one of them had a musket, which they laid down on the ground in their sight, in sign of peace, and to parley with them, but the savages would not tarry their coming. A noise of a great many more was heard behind the hill, but no more came in sight. This caused us to plant our great ordnances in places most convenient.

Wednesday, the 21st of February, the master came on shore with many of his sailors, and brought with him one of the great pieces, called a minion,[54] and helped us to draw it up the hill, with another piece that lay on shore, and mounted them, and a saller,[55] and two bases.[56] He brought with him a very fat goose to eat with us, and we had a fat crane, and a mallard, and a dried neat's[57] tongue, and so we were kindly and friendly together.

Saturday, the 3rd of March, the wind was south, the morning misty, but towards noon warm and fair weather; the birds sang in the woods most pleasantly. At one of the clock it thundered, which was the first we heard in that country; it was strong and great claps, but short, but after an hour it rained very sadly[58] till midnight.

Wednesday, the 7th of March, the wind was full east, cold, but fair. That day Master Carver with five others went to the great ponds, which seem to be excellent fishing-places; all the way they went they found it exceedingly beaten and haunted with deer, but they saw none. Amongst other fowl, they saw one a milk-white fowl, with a very black head. This day some garden seeds were sown.

Friday, the 16th, a fair warm day towards; this morning we determined to conclude of the military orders, which we had begun to consider of before but were interrupted by the savages, as we mentioned formerly. And whilst we were busied hereabout, we were interrupted again, for there presented himself a savage, which caused an alarm. He very boldly came all alone and along the houses straight to the rendezvous, where we intercepted him,[59] not suffer-

54 A cannon with 3¼ inch bore, firing a 4 pound shot.

55 Presumably a misprint for *saker*, a cannon with 4 inch bore, firing a 6 pound shot.

56 small cannons with 1¼ inch bore, firing ½ pound shot

57 beef's

58 hard; steadily

59 On first encounter, the Pilgrims were hardly hospitable to Samoset, whose friendly help in many respects was invaluable to them in later years.

ing him to go in, as undoubtedly he would, out of his bold-
ness. He saluted us in English, and bade us welcome, for
he had learned some broken English among the Englishmen
that came to fish at Monchiggon, [60] and knew by name
the most of the captains, commanders, and masters that
usually come. He was a man free in speech, so far as he
could express his mind, and of a seemly carriage. We
questioned him of many things; he was the first savage we
could meet withal. He said he was not of these parts, but
of Morattiggon,[60] and one of the sagamores or lords thereof, and had been eight months in these parts, it lying hence
a day's sail with a great wind, and five days by land. He
discoursed of the whole country, and of every province,
and of their sagamores, and their number of men, and
strength. The wind beginning to rise a little, we cast a
horseman's coat about him, for he was stark naked, only
a leather about his waist, with a fringe about a span[61] long,
or little more; he had a bow and two arrows, the one headed, and the other unheaded. He was a tall straight man,
the hair of his head black, long behind, only short before,
none on his face at all; he asked some beer, but we gave
him strong water[62] and biscuit, and butter, and cheese, and
pudding, and a piece of mallard, all which he liked well,
and had been acquainted with such amongst the English.
He told us the place where we now live is called Patuxet,
and that about four years ago all the inhabitants died of an
extraordinary plague,[63] and there is neither man, woman,
nor child remaining, as indeed we have found none, so as
there is none to hinder our possession, or to lay claim unto
it. All the afternoon we spent in communication with him;

60 Presumably, Monhegan Island, off southeastern Maine.
61 I.e., 9 inches.
62 A generic term for liquor.
63 The fact that bubonic plague had recently decimated a major
   portion of the indigenous population along the entire coast of
   New England was interpreted by the Pilgrims as divine interven-
   tion, and served as a convenient rationalization for English
   claims to the land.

we would gladly have been rid of him at night, but he was not willing to go this night. Then we thought to carry him on shipboard, wherewith he was well content, and went into the shallop, but the wind was high and the water scant, that it could not return back. We lodged him that night at Stephen Hopkin's house, and watched him.

The next day he went away back to the Massasoits,[64] from whence he said he came, who are our next bordering neighbors. They are sixty strong, as he saith. The Nausets are as near southeast of them, and are a hundred strong, and those were they of whom our people were encountered, as we before related. They are much incensed and provoked against the English, and about eight months ago slew three Englishmen, and two more hardly escaped by flight to Monchiggon; they were Sir Ferdinando Gorges his men, [65] as this savage told us, as he did likewise of the *huggery,* that is, fight, that our discoverers had with the Nausets, and of our tools that were taken out of the woods, which we willed him should be brought again, otherwise, we would right ourselves. These people are ill affected towards the English, by reason of one Hunt,[66] a master of a ship, who deceived the people, and got them under color of trucking with them, twenty out of this very place where we inhabit, and seven men from the Nausets, and carried them away, and sold them for slaves[67] like a wretched man (for twenty pound a man) that cares not what mischief he doth for his profit.

Saturday, in the morning we dismissed the savage, and gave him a knife, a bracelet, and a ring; he promised within a night or two to come again, and to bring with him some of the Massasoits, our neighbors, with such beavers' skins

64 I. e., to the Wampanoag village where Massasoit was sachem.
65 Actually members of a crew led by Capt. Thomas Dermer, on an expedition sponsored by Gorges.
66 Thomas Hunt, captain of a ship in Capt. John Smith's company.
67 (in Spain)

as they had to truck with us.

Saturday and Sunday, reasonable fair days. On this day came again the savage, and brought with him five other tall proper men; they had every man a deer's skin on him, and the principal of them had a wild cat's skin, or such like on the one arm. They had most of them long hosen[68] up to their groins, close made; and above their groins to their waist another leather, they were altogether like the Irish-trousers.[69] They are of complexion like our English gypsies, no hair or very little on their faces, on their heads long hair to their shoulders, only cut before, some trussed up before with a feather, broad-wise, like a fan, another a fox tail hanging out. These left (according to our charge given him before) their bows and arrows a quarter of a mile from our town. We gave them entertainment as we thought was fitting them; they did eat liberally of our English victuals. They made semblance unto us of friendship and amity; they sang and danced after their manner, like antics.[70] They brought with them in a thing like a bow-case (which the principal of them had about his waist) a little of their corn pounded to powder, which, put to a little water, they eat. He had a little tobacco in a bag, but none of them drank[71] but when he listed. Some of them had their faces painted black, from the forehead to the chin, four or five fingers broad; others after other fashions, as they liked. They brought three or four skins, but we would not truck with them at all that day, but wished them to bring more, and we would truck for all, which they promised within a night or two, and would leave these behind them, though we were not willing they should, and

68 leggings
69 Ireland was little better known than New England in the early seventeenth century, and comparisons between Indians and Irishmen are frequent in the descriptive accounts of English explorers of the period.
70 clowns
71 smoked

they brought us all our tools again which were taken in the woods, in our men's absence. So because of the day we dismissed them so soon as we could. But Samoset, our first acquaintance, either was sick, or feigned himself so, and would not go with them, and stayed with us till Wednesday morning. Then we sent him to them, to know the reason they came not according to their words, and we gave him a hat, a pair of stockings and shoes, a shirt, and a piece of cloth to tie about his waist.

The Sabbath day, when we sent them from us, we gave every one of them some trifles, especially the principal of them. We carried them along with our arms to the place where they left their bows and arrows, whereat they were amazed, and two of them began to slink away, but that the other called them. When they took their arrows, we bade them farewell, and they were glad, and so with many thanks given us they departed, with promise they would come again.

Monday and Tuesday proved fair days; we digged our grounds, and sowed our garden seeds.

Wednesday a fine warm day, we sent away Samoset.

That day we had again a meeting to conclude of laws and orders for ourselves, and to confirm those military orders that were formerly propounded and twice broken off by the savages' coming, but so we were again the third time, for after we had been an hour together on the top of the hill over against us two or three savages presented themselves, that made semblance of daring us, as we thought. So Captain Standish with another, with their muskets went over to them, with two of the master's mates that follow them without arms, having two muskets with them. They whetted and rubbed their arrows and strings, and made show of defiance, but when our men drew near them, they ran away; thus were we again interrupted by them. This day with much ado we got our carpenter that had been long sick of the scurvy, to fit our shallop, to fetch all from aboard.

Thursday, the 22nd of March, was a very fair warm day. About noon we met again about our public business, but we had scarce been an hour together, but Samoset came again, and Squanto, the only native of Patuxet, where we now inhabit, who was one of the twenty captives that by Hunt were carried away, and had been in England,[72] and dwelt in Cornhill with Master John Slanie, a merchant, and could speak a little English, with three others, and they brought with them some few skins to truck, and some red herrings newly taken and dried, but not salted, and signified unto us, that their great sagamore Massasoit was hard by, with Quadequina his brother, and all their men. They could not well express in English what they would, but after an hour the king came to the top of a hill over against us, and had in his train sixty men, that we could well behold them and they us. We were not willing to send our governor to them, and they unwilling to come to us, so Squanto went again unto him, who brought word that we should send one to parley with him, which we did, which was Edward Winslow, to know his mind, and to signify the mind and will of our governor, which was to have trading and peace with him. We sent to the king a pair of knives, and a copper chain with a jewel at it. To Quadequina we sent likewise a knife and a jewel to hang in his ear, and withal a pot of strong water, a good quantity of biscuit, and some butter, which were all willingly accepted.

Our messenger made a speech unto him, that King James saluted him with words of love and peace, and did accept of him as his friend and ally, and that our governor desired to see him and to truck with him, and to confirm a

---

72 The adventures of Samoset, Squanto, and other Indians who had been kidnapped and taken to Europe before whites settled in New England are recounted with accuracy and appropriate color by Carolyn T. Foreman, *Indians Abroad, 1493-1938* (Norman, 1943).

peace with him, as his next neighbor. He liked well of the
speech and heard it attentively, though the interpreters
did not well express it. After he had eaten and drunk himself, and given the rest to his company, he looked upon our
messenger's sword and armor which he had on, with in-
timation of his desire to buy it, but on the other side, our
messenger showed his unwillingness to part with it. In the
end he left him in the custody of Quadequina his brother,
and came over the brook, and some twenty men following
him, leaving all their bows and arrows behind them. We
kept six or seven as hostages for our messenger; Captain
Standish and Master Williamson[73] met the king at the
brook, with half a dozen musketeers. They saluted him
and he them, so one going over, the one on the one side, and
the other on the other, conducted him to a house then in
building, where we placed a green rug and three or four
cushions. Then instantly came our governor with drum
and trumpet after him, and some few musketeers. After
salutations, our governor kissing his hand, the king kissed
him, and so they sat down. The governor called for some
strong water, and drunk to him, and he drunk a great
draught that made him sweat all the while after; he called
for a little fresh meat, which the king did eat willingly,
and did give his followers. Then they treated of peace,
which was:

The agree-
ments of
peace
between
us and
Massasoit.

1. That neither he nor any of his should injure or do hurt
   to any of our people.

2. And if any of his did hurt to any of ours, he should
   send the offender, that we might punish him.

3. That if any of our tools were taken away when our
   people were at work, he should cause them to be re-
   stored, and if ours did any harm to any of his, we
   would do the like to them.

4. If any did unjustly war against him, we would aid

73 Presumably a misprint for *Williams*. There is no other mention of a Williamson in the early Plymouth sources.

him; if any did war against us, he should aid us.

5. He should send to his neighbor confederates, to certify them of this, that they might not wrong us, but might be likewise comprised in the conditions of peace.

6. That when their men came to us, they should leave their bows and arrows behind them, as we should do our pieces when we came to them.

Lastly, that doing thus, King James would esteem of him as his friend and ally.

All which the king seemed to like well,[74] and it was applauded of his followers; all the while he sat by the governor he trembled for fear. In his person he is a very lusty man, in his best years, an able body, grave of countenance, and spare of speech. In his attire little or nothing differing from the rest of his followers, only in a great chain of white bone beads about his neck, and at it behind ..s neck hangs a little bag of tobacco, which he drank and gave us to drink; his face was painted with a sad[75] red like murry,[76] and oiled both head and face, that he looked greasily. All his followers likewise, were in their faces, in part or in whole painted, some black, some red, some yellow, and some white, some with crosses, and other antic works; some had skins on them, and some naked, all strong, tall, all men in appearance.

So after all was done, the governor conducted him to the brook, and there they embraced each other and he departed; we diligently keeping our hostages, we expected our messenger's coming, but anon, word was brought us that Quadequina was coming, and our messenger was stayed till

74 This first American mutual security pact remained inviolate throughout Massasoit's life. He and his eldest son Wamsutta (named "Alexander" by the English) signed such a treaty in Plymouth in 1639, and it was ratified and confirmed by the colonial government. The peace was broken in 1675, for which most historians blame Wamsutta's brother and successor, Metacom ("King Philip").

75 deep

76 mulberry

his return, who presently came and a troop with him, so likewise we entertained him, and conveyed him to the place prepared. He was very fearful of our pieces, and made signs of dislike, that they should be carried away, whereupon commandment was given they should be laid away. He was a very proper tall young man, of a very modest and seemly countenance, and he did kindly like of our entertainment, so we conveyed him likewise as we did the king, but divers of their people stayed still. When he was returned, then they dismissed our messenger. Two of his people would have stayed all night, but we would not suffer it. One thing I forgot, the king had in his bosom, hanging in a string, a great long knife; he marvelled much at our trumpet, and some of his men would sound it as well as they could. Samoset and Squanto, they stayed all night with us, and the king and all his men lay all night in the woods, not above half an English mile from us, and all their wives and women with them. They said that within eight or nine days they would come and set corn on the other side of the brook, and dwell there all summer, which is hard by us. That night we kept good watch, but there was no appearance of danger.

The next morning divers of their people came over to us, hoping to get some victuals as we imagined; some of them told us the king would have some of us come see him. Captain Standish and Isaac Allerton went venturously, who were welcomed of him after their manner: he gave them three or four ground-nuts, and some tobacco. We cannot yet conceive but that he is willing to have peace with us, for they have seen our people sometimes alone two or three in the woods at work and fowling, when as they offered them no harm as they might easily have done, and especially because he hath a potent adversary the Narragansets, that are at war with him, against whom he thinks we may be some strength to him, for our pieces are terrible unto them. This morning they stayed till ten or eleven of the clock, and our governor bid them send the king's kettle, and filled it full of pease, which pleased them well, and so they went their way.

Friday was a very fair day; Samoset and Squanto still remained with us. Squanto went at noon to fish for eels; at night he came home with as many as he could well lift in one hand, which our people were glad of. They were fat and sweet; he trod them out with his feet, and so caught them with his hands without any other instrument.

This day we proceeded on with our common business, from which we had been so often hindered by the savages' coming, and concluding both of military orders and of some laws and orders as we thought behooveful for our present estate, and condition, and did likewise choose our governor for this year, which was Master John Carver, a man well approved amongst us.

A
Journey to Pokanoket,
the habitation of the great King
MASSASOIT;
as also our message, the answer and entertainment we had of him.

T seemed good to the company for many considerations to send some amongst them to Massasoit, the greatest commander amongst the savages bordering upon us; partly to know where to find them if occasion served, as also to see their strength, discover the country, prevent abuses in their disorderly coming unto us, make satisfaction for some conceived injuries to be done on our parts, and to continue the league of peace and friendship between them and us. For these, and the like ends, it pleased the governor to make choice of Stephen Hopkins and Edward Winslow to go unto him, and having a fit opportunity,[1] by reason of a savage called Squanto (that could speak English) coming unto us, with all expedition provided a horseman's coat of red cotton, and laced with a slight lace, for a present, that both they and their message might be the more acceptable amongst them.

The message was as followeth: that forasmuch as his

1 The journey to Pokanoket took place in the summer of 1621. During the preceding three months, which are unreported in this journal, Bradford notes that almost half of the settlers died in the "General Sickness." None abandoned the enterprise, however, and the *Mayflower* returned empty to England.

subjects came often and without fear, upon all occasions amongst us, so we were now come unto him, and in witness of the love and good-will the English bear unto him, the governor hath sent him a coat, desiring that the peace and amity that was between them and us might be continued, not that we feared them, but because we intended not to injure any, desiring to live peaceably, and as with all men, so especially with them, our nearest neighbors. But whereas his people came very often, and very many together unto us, bringing for the most part their wives and children with them, they were welcome; yet we being but strangers as yet at Patuxet, alias New Plymouth,[2] and not knowing how our corn might prosper, we could no longer give them such entertainment as we had done, and as we desired still to do. Yet if he would be pleased to come himself, or any special friend of his desired to see us, coming from him they should be welcome; and to the end we might know them from others, our governor had sent him a copper chain, desiring if any messenger should come from him to us, we might know him by bringing it with him, and hearken and give credit to his message accordingly. Also requesting him that such as have skins should bring them to us, and that he would hinder the multitude from oppressing us with them. And whereas at our first arrival at Paomet (called by us Cape Cod) we found there corn buried in the ground, and finding no inhabitants but some graves of

2 The derivation of this name is not clear. Six different spellings occur even within this book: *Plimoth, and New Plimoth* (both on the title page!), *Plimouth, Plimmouth, New Plimmouth,* and *New Plimmouth.* It is true that Plymouth was the town from which the settlers had finally set sail from their native country, ". . . having been kindly entertained and courteously used by divers friends there dwelling." Furthermore, the land company which granted their patent had once been called the Plymouth Company. But we need evoke neither sentimentalism nor commercial diplomacy on the part of the Pilgrims to account for the name. In fact, this site was called "Plimouth" on the map which they carried on the *Mayflower,* from Capt. John Smith's *Description of New England* (London, 1616); supposedly it was arbitrarily so designated by Prince Charles when Smith showed him a draft of the map.

dead new buried, took the corn, resolving if ever we could hear of any that had right thereunto, to make satisfaction to the full for it, yet since we understand the owners thereof were fled for fear of us, our desire was either to pay them with the like quantity of corn, English meal, or any other commodities we had to pleasure them withal; requesting him that some one of his men might signify so much unto them, and we would content him for his pains. And last of all, our governor requested one favor of him, which was, that he would exchange some of their corn for seed with us, that we might make trial which best agreed with the soil where we live.

With these presents and message we set forward the 10th June, about nine o'clock in the morning, our guide resolving that night to rest at Nemasket,[3] a town under Massasoit, and conceived by us to be very near, because the inhabitants flocked so thick upon every slight occasion amongst us; but we found it to be some fifteen English miles. On the way we found some ten or twelve men, women, and children, which had pestered us till we were weary of them, perceiving that (as the manner of them all is) where victual is easiest to be got, there they live, especially in the summer: by reason whereof, our bay affording many lobsters, they resort every spring-tide thither; and now returned with us to Nemasket. Thither we came about three o'clock after noon, the inhabitants entertaining us with joy, in the best manner they could, giving us a kind of bread called by them *maizium,* and the spawn of shads, which then they got in abundance, insomuch as they gave us spoons to eat them. With these they boiled musty acorns, but of the shads we ate heartily. After this they desired one of our men to shoot at a crow, complaining what damage they sustained in their corn by them, who shooting some fourscore off and killing, they much admired it, as other shots on other occasions.

3 Now, Middleborough, Massachusetts.

After this, Squanto told us we should hardly in one day reach Pokanoket,[4] moving us to go some eight miles further, where we should find more store and better victuals than there. Being willing to hasten our journey we went, and came thither at sunsetting, where we found many of the Namascheucks (they so calling the men of Nemasket) fishing upon a weir which they had made on a river which belonged to them, where they caught abundance of bass. These welcomed us also, gave us of their fish, and we them of our victuals, not doubting but we should have enough where'er we came. There we lodged in the open fields, for houses they had none, though they spent the most of the summer there. The head of this river is reported to be not far from the place of our abode; upon it are and have been many towns, it being a good length. The ground is very good on both sides, it being for the most part cleared. Thousands of men have lived there, which died in a great plague not long since; and pity it was and is to see so many goodly fields, and so well seated, without men to dress and manure[5] the same. Upon this river dwelleth Massasoit. It cometh into the sea at the Narraganset Bay, where the Frenchmen so much use. A ship may go many miles up it, as the savages report, and a shallop to the head of it; but so far as we saw, we are sure a shallop may.

But to return to our journey. The next morning we broke our fast, took our leave and departed, being then accompanied with some six savages. Having gone about six miles by the river side, at a known shoal place, it being low water, they spake to us to put off our breeches, for we must wade through. Here let me not forget the valor and courage of some of the savages on the opposite side of the river, for there were remaining alive only two men, both aged, especially the one being above threescore. These two, espying a company of men entering the river, ran

4 Now, the Mount Hope area of Bristol, Rhode Island.
5 cultivate; till

very swiftly and low in the grass, to meet us at the bank, where with shrill voices and great courage standing charged upon us with their bows; they demanded what we were, supposing us to be enemies, and thinking to take advantage on us in the water. But seeing we were friends, they welcomed us with such food as they had, and we bestowed a small bracelet of beads on them. Thus far we are sure the tide ebbs and flows.

Having here again refreshed ourselves we proceeded in our journey, the weather being very hot for travel, yet the country so well watered that a man could scarce be dry, but he should have a spring at hand to cool his thirst, beside small rivers in abundance. But the savages will not willingly drink but at a springhead. When we came to any small brook where no bridge was, two of them desired to carry us through of their own accords, also fearing we were or would be weary, offered to carry our pieces, also if we would lay off any of our clothes, we should have them carried; and as the one of them had found more special kindness from one of the messengers, and the other savage from the other so they showed their thankfulness accordingly in affording us all help and furtherance in the journey.

As we passed along, we observed that there were few places by the river but had been inhabited, by reason whereof much ground was clear, save of weeds which grew higher than our heads. There is much good timber, both oak, walnut tree, fir, beech, and exceeding great chestnut trees. The country, in respect of the lying of it, is both champaign and hilly, like many places in England. In some places it is very rocky both above ground and in it. And though the country be wild and overgrown with woods, yet the trees stand not thick, but a man may well ride a horse amongst them.

Passing on at length, one of the company, an Indian, espied a man and told the rest of it. We asked them if they feared any; they told us that if they were Narraganset men they would not trust them. Whereat we called for our pieces and bid them not to fear, for though they were twenty, we two alone would not care for them. But they hailing him, he proved a friend, and had only two women with him; their baskets were empty but they fetched water in their bottles, so that we drank with them and departed. After, we met another man with other two women, which had been at rendezvous by the salt water, and their baskets were full of roasted crab, fishes, and other dried shell fish, of which they gave us, and we ate and drank with them, and gave each of the women a string of beads, and departed.

After, we came to a town of Massasoit's, where we ate oysters and other fish. From thence we went to Pokanoket but Massasoit was not at home; there we stayed, he being sent for. When news was brought of his coming, our guide Squanto requested that at our meeting we would discharge our pieces. But one of us going about to charge his piece, the women and children, through fear to see him take up his piece, ran away, and could not be pacified till he laid it down again, who afterward were better informed by our interpreter.

Massasoit being come, we discharged our pieces, and saluted him, who after their manner kindly welcomed us, and took us into his house, and set us down by him, where, having delivered our foresaid message and presents, and having put the coat on his back and the chain about his neck, he was not a little proud to behold himself, and his men also to see their king so bravely[6] attired.

For answer to our message, he told us we were welcome, and he would gladly continue that peace and friendship which was between him and us, and, for his men, they should no more pester us as they had done; also that he would sent to Paomet, and would help us with corn for seed, according to our request.

6 admirably

This being done, his men gathered near to him, to whom he turned himself, and made a great speech; they sometimes interposing, and, as it were, confirming and applauding him in that he said. The meaning whereof was (as far as we could learn) thus: Was not he Massasoit, commander of the country about them? Was not such a town his, and the people of it? And should they not bring their skins unto us? To which they answered, they were his and would be at peace with us, and bring their skins to us. After this manner he named at least thirty places, and their answer was as aforesaid to every one, so that as it was delightful, it was tedious unto us.

This being ended, he lighted tobacco for us, and fell to discoursing of England, and of the King's Majesty, marvelling that he would live without a wife.[7] Also he talked of the Frenchmen, bidding us not to suffer them to come to Narraganset, for it was King James his country, and he also was King James his man. Late it grew, but victuals he offered none, for indeed he had not any, being he came so newly home. So we desired to go to rest. He laid us on the bed with himself and his wife, they at the one end and we at the other, it being only planks laid a foot from the ground, and a thin mat upon them. Two more of his chief men, for want of room, pressed by and upon us, so that we were worse weary of our lodging than of our journey.

The next day, being Thursday, many of their sachems, or petty governors, came to see us, and many of their men also. There they went to their manner of games for skins and knives. There we challenged them to shoot with them for skins, but they durst not; only they desired to see one of us shoot at a mark, who shooting with hail-shot, they wondered to see the mark so full of holes.

About one o'clock, Massasoit brought two fishes that he had shot; they were like bream but three times so big, and

7 The wife of James I had died more than a year before the Pilgrims sailed from England.

better meat. These being boiled there were at least forty looked for share in them, the most ate of them. This meal only we had in two nights and a day, and had not one of us bought a partridge we had taken our journey fasting. Very importunate he was to have us stay with them longer. But we desired to keep the Sabbath at home, and feared we should either be light-headed for want of sleep, for what with bad lodging, the savages' barbarous singing (for they use to sing themselves asleep), lice and fleas within doors, and mosquitoes without, we could hardly sleep all the time of our being there; we much fearing that if we should stay any longer, we should not be able to recover home for want of strength. So that on the Friday morning before sunrising, we took our leave and departed, Massasoit being both grieved and ashamed that he could no better entertain us, and retaining Squanto to send from place to place to procure truck for us, and appointing another, called Tokamahamon, in his place, whom we had found faithful before and after upon all occasions.

At this town of Massasoit's where we before ate, we were again refreshed with a little fish, and bought about a handful of meal of their parched corn, which was very precious at that time of the year, and a small string of dried shell-fish, as big as oysters. The latter we gave to the six savages that accompanied us, keeping the meal for ourselves. When we drank, we ate each a spoonful of it with a pipe of tobacco, instead of other victuals, and of this also we could not but give them so long as it lasted. Five miles they led us to a house out of the way in hope of victuals, but we found nobody there and so were but worse able to return home. That night we reached to the weir where we lay before, but the Namascheucks were returned, so that we had no hope of any thing there. One of the savages had shot a shad in the water, and a small squirrel as big as a rat, called a *neuxis;* the one half of either he gave us, and after went to the weir to fish. From hence we wrote to

Plymouth, and sent Tokamahamon before to Nemasket, willing him from thence to send another, that he might meet us with food at Nemasket. Two men now only remained with us, and it pleased God to give them good store of fish, so that we were well refreshed. After supper we went to rest, and they to fishing again; more they got and fell to eating afresh, and retained sufficient ready roast for all our breakfasts. About two o'clock in the morning arose a great storm of wind, rain, lightning, and thunder, in such violent manner that we could not keep in our fire, and had the savages not roasted fish when we were asleep, we had set forward fasting, for the rain still continued with great violence, even the whole day through, till we came within two miles of home.

Being wet and weary, at length we came to Nemasket; there we refreshed ourselves, giving gifts to all such as had showed us any kindness. Amongst others, one of the six that came with us from Pokanoket, having before this on the way unkindly foresaken us, marvelled we gave him nothing, and told us what he had done for us. We also told him of some discourtesies he offered us, whereby he deserved nothing. Yet we gave him a small trifle, whereupon he offered us tobacco; but the house being full of people, we told them he stole some by the way, and if it were of that we would not take it, for we would not receive that which was stolen upon any terms; if we did, our God would be angry with us, and destroy us. This abashed him and gave the rest great content. But at our departure he would needs carry him on his back through a river, whom he had formerly in some sort abused. Fain they would have had us to lodge there all night, and wondered we would set forth again in such weather. But, God be praised, we came safe home that night, though wet, weary, and surbated.[8]

8 fatigued; bruised

A
VOYAGE MADE BY TEN
of our men to the Kingdom of Nauset,
to seek a boy that had lost
himself in the woods;
with such accidents
as befell us in that
voyage.

He 11th of June we set forth, the weather being very fair. But ere we had been long at sea, there arose a storm of wind and rain, with much lightning and thunder, insomuch that a spout arose not far from us, but, God be praised, it dured not long, and we put in that night for harbor at a place called Cummaquid,[1] where we had some hope to find the boy. Two savages were in the boat with us, the one was Squanto, our interpreter, the other Tokamahamon, a special friend. It being night before we came in, we anchored in the midst of the bay, where we were dry at alow water. In the morning we espied savages seeking lobsters, and sent our two interpreters to speak with them, the channel being between them; where they told them what we were, and for what we were come, willing them not at all to fear us, for we would not hurt them. Their answer was, that the boy was well, but he was at Nauset;[2] yet since we were there they desired us to come ashore and eat with them; which, as soon as our boat

1 Now, Barnstable, Massachusetts.
2 Now, Eastham, Massachusetts.

floated, we did, and went six ashore, having four pledges for them in the boat. They brought us to their sachem or governor, whom they call Iyanough, a man not exceeding twenty-six years of age, but very personable, gentle, courteous, and fair conditioned, indeed not like a savage, save for his attire. His entertainment was answerable to his parts, and his cheer plentiful and various.

One thing was very grievous unto us at this place. There was an old woman, whom we judged to be no less than a hundred years old, which came to see us because she never saw English, yet could not behold us without breaking forth into great passion, weeping and crying excessively. We demanding the reason of it, they told us she had three sons who, when Master Hunt was in these parts, went aboard his ship to trade with him, and he carried them captives into Spain (for Squanto at that time was carried away also) by which means she was deprived of the comfort of her children in her old age. We told them we were sorry that any Englishman should give them that offense, that Hunt was a bad man, and that all the English that heard of it condemned him for the same; but for us, we would not offer them any such injury though it would gain us all the skins in the country. So we gave her some small trifles, which somewhat appeased her.

After dinner we took boat for Nauset, Iyanough and two of his men accompanying us. Ere we came to Nauset, the day and tide were almost spent, insomuch as we could not go in with our shallop, but the sachem or governor of Cummaquid went ashore and his men with him. We also sent Squanto to tell Aspinet, the sachem of Nauset, wherefore we came. The savages here came very thick amongst us, and were earnest with us to bring in our boat. But we neither well could, nor yet desired to do it, because we had least cause to trust them, being they only had formerly made an assault upon us in the same place, in time of our winter discovery for habitation. And indeed it was no marvel they did so, for howsoever, through snow or otherwise, we saw no houses, yet we were in the midst of them.

When our boat was aground they came very thick, but we stood therein upon our guard, not suffering any to enter except two, the one being of Manomoyik,[3] and one of those whose corn we had formerly found; we promised him restitution, and desired him either to come to Patuxet for satisfaction, or else we would bring them so much corn again. He promised to come; we used him very kindly for the present. Some few skins we got there but not many.

After sunset, Aspinet came with a great train, and brought the boy with him, one bearing him through the water. He had not less than a hundred with him, the half whereof came to the shallop side unarmed with him, the other stood aloof with their bows and arrows. There he delivered us the boy, behung with beads, and made peace with us, we bestowing a knife on him, and likewise on another that first entertained the boy and brought him thither. So they departed from us.

Here we understood that the Narragansets had spoiled[4] some of Massasoit's men, and taken him. This struck some fear in us, because the colony was so weakly guarded, the strength thereof being abroad. But we set forth with resolution to make the best haste home we could; yet the wind being contrary, having scarce any fresh water left, and at least sixteen leagues home, we put in again for the shore. There we met again with Iyanough, the sachem of Cummaquid, and the most of his town, both men, women, and children with him. He, being still willing to gratify us, took a runlet[5] and led our men in the dark a great way for water, but could find none good, yet brought such as there was on his neck with him. In the meantime the

3 Now, Chatham, Massachusetts.
4 In early seventeenth-century usage, this could imply anything from disarming to kidnapping, from robbing to killing.
5 small keg

women joined hand in hand, singing and dancing before the shallop, the men also showing all the kindness they could, Iyanough himself taking a bracelet from about his neck and hanging it upon one of us.

Again we set out, but to small purpose, for we gat but little homeward.

Our water also was very brackish, and not to be drunk. The next morning. Iyanough espied us again and ran after us; we, being resolved to go to Cummaquid again to water, took him into the shallop, whose entertainment was not inferior unto the former.

The soil at Nauset and here is alike, even and sandy, not so good for corn as where we are. Ships may safely ride in either harbor. In the summer they abound with fish. Being now watered we put forth again, and, by God's providence, came safely home that night.

A
JOURNEY TO THE
Kingdom of Nemasket
in defense of the great King
Massasoit, against the Narragansets,
and to revenge the supposed
death of our interpreter
Squanto.

AT our return from Nauset, we found it true that Massasoit was put from his country by the Narragansets. Word also was brought unto us that Corbitant, a petty sachem or governor under Massasoit (whom they ever feared to be too conversant with the Narragansets), was at Nemasket, who sought to draw the hearts of Massasoit's subjects from him, speaking also disdainfully of us, storming at the peace between Nauset, Cummaquid, and us, and at Squanto, the worker of it; also at Tokamahamon, and one Hobomok (two Indians, or Lemes,[1] one of which he would treacherously have murdered a little before, being a special and trusty man of Massasoit's). Tokamahamon went to him, but the other two would not, yet put their lives in their hands, privately went to see if they could hear of their king, and lodging at Nemasket were discovered to Corbitant, who set a guard to beset the house, and took Squanto (for he had said, if he were dead

---

1 This passage defies interpretation. "Or Lemes" has no sense in seventeenth-century English or local Indian languages. Most previous editors have assumed this to be a misprint for *our allies;* I am not altogether happy with that interpretation but have nothing better to offer.

73

the English had lost their tongue). Hobomok, seeing that Squanto was taken, and Corbitant held a knife at his breast, being a strong and stout man, broke from them and came to New Plymouth, full of fear and sorrow for Squanto, whom he thought to be slain.

Upon this news the company assembled together, and resolved on the morrow to send ten men armed to Nemasket, and Hobomok for their guide, to revenge the supposed death of Squanto on Corbitant our bitter enemy, and to retain Nepeof, another sachem or governor, who was of this confederacy, till we heard what was become of our friend Massasoit.

On the morrow we set out ten men armed, who took their journey as aforesaid, but the day proved very wet. When we supposed we were within three or four miles of Nemasket, we went out of the way and stayed there till night, because we would not be discovered. There we consulted what to do, and thinking best to beset the house at midnight, each was appointed his task by the captain, all men encouraging one another to the utmost of their power. By night our guide lost his way, which much discouraged our men, being we were wet, and weary of our arms, but one of our men, having been before at Nemasket, brought us into the way again.

Before we came to the town, we sat down and ate such as our knapsacks afforded. That being done, we threw them aside, and all such things as might hinder us, and so went on and beset the house, according to our last resolution. Those that entered demanded if Corbitant were not there, but fear had bereft the savages of speech. We charged them not to stir, for if Corbitant were not there, we would not meddle with them; if he were, we came principally for him, to be avenged on him for the supposed death of Squanto, and other matters; but, howsoever, we would not at all hurt their women or children. Notwithstanding, some of them pressed out at a private door and escaped, but with some wounds. At length perceiving our principal ends, they told us Corbitant was returned with all his train, and that Squanto was yet living, and in the town, offering some tobacco, other such as they had to eat. In this hurly-burly we discharged two pieces at random, which much terrified all the inhabitants, except Squanto and Tokamahamon, who, though they knew not our end in coming, yet assured them of our honesty, that we would not hurt them. Those boys that were in the house, seeing our care of women, often cried, *"Neen squaes,"* that is to say, "I am a woman"; the women also hanging upon Hobomok, calling him *Towam,* that is, "friend." But to be short, we kept them we had, and made them make a fire that we might see to search the house. In the meantime Hobomok got on the top of the house and called Squanto and Tokamahamon, which came unto us accompanied with others, some armed and others naked. Those that had bows and arrows, we took them away, promising them again when it was day. The house we took for our better safeguard, but released those we had taken, manifesting whom we came for and wherefore.

On the next morning we marched into the midst of the town, and went to the house of Squanto to breakfast. Thither came all whose hearts were upright towards us, but all Corbitant's faction were fled away. There in the midst of them we manifested again our intendment, assuring them, that although Corbitant had now escaped us, yet there was no place should secure him and his from us if he continued his threatening us and provoking others against us, who had kindly entertained him, and never intended evil towards him till he now so justly deserved it. Moreover, if Massasoit did not return in safety from Narraganset, or if hereafter he should make any insurrection against him, or offer violence to Squanto, Hobomok, or any of Massasoit's subjects, we would revenge it upon him, to the overthrow of him and his. As for those were wounded, we were sorry for it, though themselves procured it in not staying in the house at our command; yet if they would return home with us, our surgeon should heal them.

At this offer, one man and a woman that were wounded went home with us, Squanto and many other known friends accompanying us, and offering all help that might be by carriage of any thing we had to ease us. So that, by God's good providence, we safely returned home the morrow night after we set forth.

A
RELATION OF OUR
Voyage to the Massachusets,
and what happened there.

T seemed good to the company in general, that though the Massachusets had often threatened us (as we were informed), yet we should go amongst them, partly to see the country, partly to make peace with them, and partly to procure their truck. For these ends the governors chose ten men fit for the purpose, and sent Squanto and two other savages to bring us to speech with the people, and interpret for us.

We set out about midnight,[1] the tide then serving for us. We supposing it to be nearer than it is, thought to be there the next morning betimes, but it proved well near twenty leagues from New Plymouth.

We came into the bottom of the bay,[2] but being late we anchored and lay in the shallop, not having seen any of the people. The next morning we put in for the shore. There we found many lobsters that had been gathered together by the savages, which we made ready under a cliff. The captain set two sentinels behind the cliff to the landward to secure the shallop, and taking a guide with him and four of our company, went to seek the inhabitants; where they met a woman coming for her lobsters, they told her of them, and contented her for them. She told them where the people were. Squanto went to them; the rest returned,

1 Bradford's *Of Plymouth Plantation* sets the date of this embarkation as 18 September 1621.
2 I. e., Boston Harbor.

having direction which way to bring the shallop to them.

The sachem or governor of this place, is called Obbatine-wat, and though he lives in the bottom of the Massachusetts Bay, yet he is under Massasoit. He used us very kindly; he told us he durst not then remain in any settled place, for fear of the Tarentines.[3] Also the Squaw Sachem,[4] or Massachusets' queen, was an enemy to him.

We told him of divers sachems that had acknowledged themselves to be King James his men, and if he also would submit himself, we would be his safeguard from his enemies, which he did, and went along with us to bring us to the Squaw Sachem. Again we crossed the bay, which is very large and hath at least fifty islands in it, but the certain number is not known to the inhabitants. Night it was before we came to that side of the bay where this people were. On shore the savages went but found nobody. That night also we rid at anchor aboard the shallop.

On the morrow we went ashore, all but two men, and marched in arms up in the country. Having gone three miles we came to a place where corn had been newly gather-ed, a house pulled down, and the people gone. A mile from hence, Nanepashemet, their king, in his life-time had lived. His house was not like others, but a scaffold was largely built, with poles and planks some six feet from ground, and the house upon that, being situated on the top of a hill.

Not far from hence, in a bottom, we came to a fort built by their deceased king, the manner thus: there were poles some thirty or forty feet long, stuck in the ground as thick as they could be set one by another, and with these they enclosed a ring some forty of fifty feet over. A trench breast high was digged on each side; one way there was to go into it with a bridge; in the midst of this palisade stood the frame of a house wherein, being dead, he lay buried.

About a mile from hence, we came to such another, but

3 Presumably, the Abnaki, an Algonquian tribe of eastern Maine.
4 Presumably, the widow of Nanepashemet.

seated on the top of a hill; here Nanepashemet was killed, none dwelling in it since the time of his death. At this place we stayed, and sent two savages to look the inhabitants, and to inform them of our ends in coming, that they might not be fearful of us. Within a mile of this place they found the women of the place together, with their corn on heaps, whither we supposed them to be fled for fear of us, and the more, because in divers places they had newly pulled down their houses, and for haste in one place had left some of their corn covered with a mat, and nobody with it.

With much fear they entertained us at first, but seeing our gentle carriage towards them, they took heart and entertained us in the best manner they could, boiling cod and such other things as they had for us. At length, with much sending for, came one of their men, shaking and trembling for fear. But when he saw we intended them no hurt, but came to truck, he promised us his skins also. Of him we inquired for their queen, but it seemed she was far from thence—at least we could not see her.

Here Squanto would have had us rifle the savage women, and taken their skins and all such things as might be serviceable for us; for (said he) they are a bad people, and have oft threatened you. But our answer was: Were they never so bad, we would not wrong them, or give them any just occasion against us; for their words, we little weighed them, but if they once attempted any thing against us, then we would deal far worse than he desired.

Having well spent the day, we returned to the shallop, almost all the women accompanying us to truck, who sold their coats from their backs, and tied boughs about them, but with great shamefacedness (for indeed they are more modest than some of our English women are). We promised them to come again to them, and they us, to keep their skins.

Within this bay the savages say there are two rivers, the one whereof we saw, having a fair entrance, but we had no time to discover it. Better harbors for shipping cannot be than here are. At the entrance of the bay are many rocks, and in all likelihood very good fishing-ground. Many, yea, most of the islands have been inhabited, some being cleared from end to end, but the people are all dead, or removed.

Our victual growing scarce, the wind coming fair, and having a light moon, we set out at evening and, through the goodness of God, came safely home before noon the day following.

A
LETTER SENT FROM
New England to a friend in these parts,
setting forth a brief and true declaration
of the worth of that plantation;
as also certain useful directions
for such as intend a voyage
into those parts.

Loving and Old Friend,[1]

Although I received no letter from you by this ship,[2] yet forasmuch as I know you expect the performance of my promise, which was, to write unto you truly and faithfully of all things, I have therefore at this time sent unto you accordingly, referring you for further satisfaction to our more large relations.[3]

You shall understand that in this little time that a few of us have been here, we have built seven dwelling-houses, and four for the use of the plantation, and have made preparation for divers others. We set the last spring some twenty acres of Indian corn, and sowed some six acres of

---

1 The following appears to be a covering letter which may have accompanied the manuscript journal when it was sent from Plymouth. Perhaps the "loving and old friend" of the author is George Morton, who presumably edited the relations for publication. See Introduction.

2 The *Fortune*, first to follow the *Mayflower*.

3 I. e., the preceding five narratives.

barley and pease, and according to the manner of the Indians, we manured our ground with herrings, or rather shads, which we have in great abundance, and take with great ease at our doors. Our corn did prove well, and, God be praised, we had a good increase of Indian corn, and our barley indifferent good, but our pease not worth the gathering, for we feared they were too late sown. They came up very well, and blossomed, but the sun parched them in the blossom.

Our harvest being gotten in, our governor sent four men on fowling, that so we might after a special manner rejoice together after we had gathered the fruit of our labors.[4] They four in one day killed as much fowl as, with a little help beside, served the company almost a week. At which time, amongst other recreations, we exercised our arms, many of the Indians coming amongst us, and among the rest their greatest king Massasoit, with some ninety men, whom for three days we entertained and feasted, and they went out and killed five deer, which they brought to the plantation and bestowed on our governor, and upon the captain and others. And although it be not always so plentiful as it was at this time with us, yet by the goodness of God, we are so far from want that we often wish you partakers of our plenty.

We have found the Indians very faithful in their covenant of peace with us, very loving and ready to pleasure us. We often go to them, and they come to us; some of us have been fifty miles by land in the country with them, the occasions and relations whereof you shall understand by our general and more full declaration of such things as are worth the noting. Yea, it hath pleased God so to possess the Indians with a fear of us, and love unto us, that not

---

4 The following is the earliest description of the first Thanksgiving. The dates are not specified, nor is there specific mention of turkeys as comprising part of the feast, although they doubtless did.

only the greatest king amongst them, called Massasoit, but also all the princes and peoples round about us, have either made suit unto us, or been glad of any occasion to make peace with us, so that seven of them at once have sent their messengers to us to that end.[5] Yea, an Fle[6] at sea, which we never saw, hath also, together with the former, yielded willingly to be under the protection, and subjects to our sovereign lord King James. So that there is now great peace amongst the Indians themselves, which was not formerly, neither would have been but for us; and we for our parts walk as peaceably and safely in the wood as in the highways in England. We entertain them familiarly in our houses, and they as friendly bestowing their venison on us. They are a people without any religion or knowledge of any God, yet very trusty, quick of apprehension, ripe-witted, just. The men and women go naked, only a skin about their middles.

For the temper of the air, here it agreeth well with that in England, and if there be any difference at all, this is somewhat hotter in summer. Some think it to be colder in winter, but I cannot out of experience so say; the air is very clear and not foggy, as hath been reported. I never in my life remember a more seasonable year than we have here enjoyed, and if we have once but kine, horses, and sheep,

5 The author here probably refers to the following document which was printed in 1669, in Morton's *New England's Memorial*:

"September 13, Anno Dom. 1621.
"Know all men by these presents, that we whose names are underwritten do acknowledge ourselves to be the loyal subjects of King James, King of Great Britain, France, and Ireland, Defender of the Faith, &c. In witness whereof, and as a testimonial of the same, we have subscribed our names or marks, as followeth:
Ohquamehud, Cawnacome, Obbatinnua, Nattawahunt, Caunbatant, Chikkatabak, Quadequina, Huttamoiden, Apannow.
6 No such word occurs in either seventeenth-century English or local Indian languages. It is presumably a misprint for "Ile," i.e., *isle,* referring to Martha's Vineyard.

I make no question but men might live as contented here as in any part of the world. For fish and fowl, we have great abundance; fresh cod in the summer is but coarse meat with us; our bay is full of lobsters all the summer and affordeth variety of other fish; in September we can take a hogshead of eels in a night, with small labor, and can dig them out of their beds all the winter. We have mussels and othus[7] at our doors. Oysters we have none near, but we can have them brought by the Indians when we will; all the spring-time the earth sendeth forth naturally very good sallet herbs.[8] Here are grapes, white and red, and very sweet and strong also. Strawberries, gooseberries, raspas,[9] etc. Plums of three sorts, with black and red, being almost as good as a damson; abundance of roses, white, red, and damask; single, but very sweet indeed. The country wanteth only industrious men to employ, for it would grieve your hearts if, as I, you had seen so many miles together by goodly rivers uninhabited, and withal, to consider those parts of the world wherein you live to be even greatly burdened with abundance of people. These things I thought good to let you understand, being the truth of things as near as I could experimentally take knowledge of, and that you might on our behalf give God thanks who hath dealt so favorably with us.

Our supply of men[10] from you came the 9th of November 1621, putting in at Cape Cod, some eight or ten leagues

7 This also defies identification. Perhaps it is a misprint for *others.*

8 I.e., salad greens.

9 raspberries

10 Thirty-five new settlers arrived on the *Fortune,* of whom some had set out with the original party but had to return to Plymouth, England, with the disabled ship *Speedwell.* The newly arrived heads of family were (in alphabetical order):
John Adams, William Basset, William Beale, Edward Bompasse, Jonathan Brewster, Clement Briggs, John Cannon, Wil-

from us. The Indians that dwell thereabout were they who were owners of the corn which we found in caves, for which we have given them full content, and are in great league with them. They sent us word there was a ship near unto them, but thought it to be a Frenchman, and indeed for ourselves, we expected not a friend so soon. But when we perceived that she made for our bay, the governor commanded a great piece to be shot off, to call home such as were abroad at work; where-upon every man, yea, boy, that could handle a gun, were ready, with full resolution that if she were an enemy, we would stand in our just defense, not fearing them, but God provided better for us than we supposed. These came all in health, not any being sick by the way (otherwise than by sea-sickness) and so continue at this time, by the blessing of God; the good-wife Ford was delivered of a son the first night she landed, and both of them are very well.

When it pleaseth God, we are settled and fitted for the fishing business, and other trading; I doubt not but by the blessing of God the gain will give content to all. In the mean time, that we have gotten we have sent by this ship,[11] and though it be not much, yet it will witness for us that

---

liam Conner, Thomas Cushman, Stephen Dean, Philip de la Noye, Thomas Flavell, Widow Ford, Robert Hicks, William Hilton, Bennet Morgan, Thomas Morton, Austin Nicholas, William Palmer, William Pitt, Thomas Prence, Moses Simonson, Hugh Stacie, James Stewart, William Tench, John Winslow, William Wright.

Also aboard was Robert Cushman who presumably carried the manuscript journal back to England with him on the *Fortune's* return trip a month later.

11 Bradford's *Of Plymouth Plantation* describes the *Fortune's* cargo as comprising beaver skins, clapboards, and sassafras, all of which was stolen by French privateers shortly before her arrival in London.

we have not been idle, considering the smallness of our number all this summer. We hope the merchants will accept of it, and be encouraged to furnish us with things needful for further employment, which will also encourage us to put forth ourselves to the uttermost.

Now because I expect your coming unto us[12] with other of our friends, whose company we much desire, I thought good to advertise[13] you of a few things needful. Be careful to have a very good bread-room to put your biscuits in. Let your cask for beer and water be iron-bound for the first tire if not more; let not your meat be dry-salted—none can better do it than the sailors. Let your meal be so hard trod in your cask that you shall need an adz or hatchet to work it out with. Trust not too much on us for corn at this time, for by reason of this last company that came, depending wholly upon us, we shall have little enough till harvest; be careful to come by some of your meal to spend by the way—it will much refresh you. Build your cabins as open as you can, and bring good store of clothes and bedding with you. Bring every man a musket or fowling-piece; let your piece be long in the barrel, and fear not the weight of it, for most of our shooting is from stands. Bring juice of lemons, and take it fasting; it is of good use. For hot waters, aniseed water is the best, but use it sparingly. If you bring any thing for comfort in the country, butter or sallet oil, or both is very good. Our Indian corn, even the coarsest, maketh as pleasant meat as rice, therefore spare that unless to spend by the way; bring paper and linseed oil for your windows, with cotton yarn for your lamps. Let your shot be most for big fowls, and bring store of powder and shot. I forbear further to write for the present,

12 George Morton, to whom this letter was presumably written, did come with the next party, on the ship *Anne*.
13 advise

hoping to see you by the next return, so I take my leave, commending you to the Lord for a safe conduct unto us. Resting in him,

Your loving friend,

E. W.[14]

Plymouth, in New England, this 11th of December, 1621.

14 Presumably, Edward Winslow. See Introduction.

Reasons and Considerations touching
the lawfulness of removing out of
England into the parts of America.

Orasmuch as many exceptions are daily made against the going into and inhabiting of foreign desert places, to the hindrances of plantations abroad, and the increase of distractions at home, it is not amiss that some which have been ear-witnesses of the exceptions made, and are either agents or abettors of such removals and plantations, do seek to give content to the world, in all things that possibly they can.

The Preamble

And although the most of the opposites are such as either dream of raising their fortunes here,[1] to that than which there is nothing more unlike, or such as affecting their home-born country so vehemently, as that they had rather with all their friends beg, yea, starve in it, than undergo a little difficulty in seeking abroad; yet are there some who, out of doubt in tenderness of conscience, and fear to offend God by running before they be called, are straitened and do straiten others from going to foreign plantations.

For whose cause especially, I have been drawn, out of my good affection to them, to publish some reasons that might give them content and satisfaction, and also stay and stop the wilful and witty caviller; and herein I trust I shall not be blamed of any godly wise, though through my slender judgment I should miss the mark, and not strike the nail on the head, considering it is the first attempt that hath been made (that I know of) to defend those enterprises. Reason would, therefore, that if any man of deeper

1 I.e., in England.

88

reach and better judgment see further or otherwise, that he rather instruct me than deride me.

And being studious for brevity, we must first consider that whereas God of old did call and summon our fathers Cautions by predictions, dreams, visions, and certain illuminations to Gen. 12:1,2, go from their countries, places, and habitations, to reside & 35:1. and dwell here or there, and to wander up and down from city to city, and land to land, according to his will and pleasure, now there is no such calling to be expected Matt. 2:19. for any matter whatsoever, neither must any so much as imagine that there will now be any such thing. God did Ps. 105:13. once so train up his people, but now he doth not, but speaks in another manner, and so we must apply ourselves to Heb. 1:1,2. God's present dealing, and not to his wonted dealing; and Josh. 5:12. as the miracle of giving manna ceased when the fruits of the land became plenty, so God, having such a plentiful storehouse of directions in his holy word, there must not now any extraordinary revelations be expected. But now the ordinary examples and precepts of the Scriptures, reasonably and rightly understood and applied, must be the voice and word that must call us, press us, and direct us in every action.

Neither is there any land or possession now, like unto the possession which the Jews had in Canaan, being legally Gen. 17:8. holy and appropriated unto a holy people, the seed of Abraham, in which they dwelt securely and had their days prolonged, it being by an immediate voice said, that he (the Lord) gave it them as a land of rest after their weary travels, and a type of eternal rest in heaven but now there is no land of that sanctimony, no land so appropriated, none typical, much less any that can be said to be given of God to any nation as was Canaan, which they and their seed must dwell in, till God sendeth upon them sword or captivity. But now we are all in all places strangers and pilgrims, travellers and sojourners, most properly, having no dwelling but in this earthen tabernacle; our dwelling is but a wandering, and our abiding but as a fleeting, and

II Cor. 5:1, 2,3.

in a word our home is nowhere, but in the heavens, in that house not made with hands, whose maker and builder is

So were the Jews, but yet their temporal blessings and inheritances were more large than ours.

God, and to which all ascend that love the coming of our Lord Jesus.

Though then there may be reasons to persuade a man to live in this or that land, yet there cannot be the same reasons which the Jews had, but now as natural, civil and religious bands tie men, so they must be bound, and as good reasons for things terrene and heavenly appear, so they must

Object.

be led. And so here falleth in our question, how a man that is here born and bred, and hath lived some years, may remove himself into another country.

I answer, a man must not respect only to live, and do

Answ. 1. What persons may hence remove.

good to himself, but he should see where he can live to do most good to others; for, as one saith, "He whose living is but for himself, it is time he were dead." Some men there are who of necessity must here live, as being tied to duties, either to church, commonwealth, household, kindred, etc. But others, and that many, who do no good in none of those, nor can do none, as being not able, or not in favor, or as wanting opportunity, and live as outcasts, nobodies, eye-sores, eating but for themselves, teaching but themselves, and doing good to none, either in soul or body, and so pass over days, years, and months, yea, so live and so die. Now such should lift up their eyes and see whether there be not some other place and country to which they may go to do good and have use towards others of that knowledge, wisdom, humanity, reason, strength, skill, faculty, etc., which

2. Why they should remove.

God hath given them for the service of others and his own glory.

But not to pass the bounds of modesty so far as to name

Luke 19:20.

any, though I confess I know many, who sit here still with their talent in a napkin, having notable endowments both of body and mind, and might do great good if they were in some places, which here do none, nor can do none, and yet through fleshly fear, niceness,[2] straitness of heart, etc., sit still and look on and will not hazard a dram of health, nor a day of pleasure, nor an hour of rest to further the knowledge and salvation of the sons of Adam in that New World, **Reas. 1.** where a drop of the knowledge of Christ is most precious, which is here not set by. Now what shall we say to such a profession of Christ, to which is joined no more denial of a man's self?

But some will say, what right have I to go live in the heathens' country? **Object.**

Letting pass the ancient discoveries, contracts and agree- **Answ.** ments which our Englishmen have long since made in those parts, together with the acknowledgment of the histories and chronicles of other nations, who profess the land of America from the Cape de Florida unto the Bay of Canada (which is south and north three hundred leagues and upwards, and east and west further than yet hath been discovered) is· proper to the King of England—yet letting that pass, lest I be thought to meddle further than it concerns me, or further than I have discerning, I will mention such things as are within my reach, knowledge, sight and practise, since I have travailed in these affairs.

And first, seeing we daily pray for the conversion of the **Reas. 2.** heathens, we must consider whether there be not some ordinary means and course for us to take to convert them, or whether prayer for them be only referred to God's extraordinary work from heaven. Now it seemeth unto me that we ought also to endeavor and use the means to convert them, and the means cannot be used unless we go to them or they come to us; to us they cannot come, our land is full; to them we may go, their land is empty.

This then is a sufficient reason to prove our going thither **Reas. 3.** to live lawful: their land is spacious and void, and there are few and do but run over the grass, as do also the foxes and wild beasts. They are not industrious, neither have

2 shyness

art, science, skill or faculty to use either the land or the commodities of it, but all spoils, rots, and is marred for want of manuring, gathering, ordering, etc. As the ancient patriarchs therefore removed from straiter places into more roomy, where the land lay idle and waste, and none used it, though there dwelt inhabitants by them, (as Gen. 13:6,11,12, and 34:21, and 41:20), so is it lawful now to take a land which none useth, and make use of it.

Reas. 4.
This is to be considered as respecting New England, and the territories about the plantation.

And as it is a common land or unused, and undressed country, so we have it by common consent, composition and agreement, which agreement is double. First, the imperial governor Massasoit, whose circuits in likelihood are larger than England and Scotland, hath acknowledged the King's Majesty of England to be his master and commander, and that once in my hearing, yea, and in writing, under his hand to Captain Standish, both he and many other kings which are under him, as Paomet, Nauset, Cummaquid, Narraganset, Nemasket, etc., with divers others that dwell about the bays of Patuxet and Massachusetts. Neither hath this been accomplished by threats and blows, or shaking of sword and sound of trumpet, for as our faculty that way is small, and our strength less, so our warring with them is after another manner, namely by friendly usage, love, peace, honest and just carriages, good counsel, etc., that so we and they may not only live in peace in that land, and they yield subjection to an earthly prince, but that as voluntaries they may be persuaded at length to embrace the Prince of Peace, Christ Jesus, and rest in peace with him forever.

Pss. 110:3, & 48:3.

Secondly, this composition is also more particular and applicatory, as touching ourselves there inhabiting: the emperor, by a joint consent, hath promised and appointed us to live at peace where we will in all his dominions, taking what place we will, and as much land as we will, and bringing as many people as we will, and that for these two causes. First, because we are the servants of James, King of England, whose the land (as he confesseth) is; second, because he hath found us just, honest, kind and peaceable, and so loves our company; yea, and that in these things there is no dissimulation on his part, nor fear of breach (except our security engender in them some unthought of treachery, or our uncivility provoke them to anger) is most plain in other relations,[3] which show that the things they did were more out of love than out of fear.

It being then, first, a vast and empty chaos; secondly, acknowledged the right of our sovereign king; thirdly, by a peaceable composition in part possessed of divers of his loving subjects, I see not who can doubt or call in question the lawfulness of inhabiting or dwelling there, but that it may be as lawful for such as are not tied upon some special occasion here, to live there as well as here. Yea, and as the enterprise is weighty and difficult, so the honor is more worthy, to plant a rude wilderness, to enlarge the honor and fame of our dread sovereign, but chiefly to display the efficacy and power of the Gospel, both in zealous preaching, professing, and wise walking under it, before the faces of these poor blind infidels.

As for such as object the tediousness of the voyage thither, the danger of pirates' robbery, of the savages' treachery, etc., these are but lions in the way, and it were well for such men if they were in heaven, for who can show them a place in this world where iniquity shall not compass them at the heels, and where they shall have a day without grief, or a lease of life for a moment; and who can tell, but God, what dangers may lie at our doors, even in our native country, or what plots may be abroad, or when God will cause our sun to go down at noon-days, and in the midst of our peace and security, lay upon us some lasting scourge for our so long neglect and contempt of his most glorious Gospel?

But we have here great peace, plenty of the Gospel, and

Prov. 22:13.

Ps. 49:5.

Matt. 6:34.

Amos 8:9.

Ob.

3 That is, the preceding journal.

many sweet delights, and variety of comforts.

II Chron. 32:25.

Gen. 13:9, 10.

True indeed, and far be it from us to deny and diminish the least of these mercies, but have we rendered unto God thankful obedience for this long peace, whilst other peoples have been at wars? Have we not rather murmured, repined, and fallen at jars amongst ourselves, whilst our peace hath lasted with foreign power? Was there ever more suits in law, more envy, contempt and reproach than nowadays? Abraham and Lot departed asunder when there fell a breach betwixt them, which was occasioned by the straitness of the land; and surely, I am persuaded that howsoever the frailties of men are principal in all contentions, yet the straitness of the place is such as each man is fain to pluck his means, as it were, out of his neighbor's throat; there is such pressing and oppressing in town and country, about farms, trades, traffic, etc., so as a man can hardly any where set up a trade but he shall pull down two of his neighbors.

The towns abound with young tradesmen, and the hospitals are full of the ancient; the country is replenished with new farmers, and the almshouses are filled with old laborers; many there are who get their living with bearing burdens, but more are fain to burden the land with their whole bodies. Multitudes get their means of life by prating, and so do numbers more by begging. Neither come these straits upon men always through intemperance, ill husbandry, indiscretion, etc., as some think, but even the most wise, sober, and discreet men go often to the wall, when they have done their best, wherein, as God's providence swayeth all, so it is easy to see that the straitness of the place, having in it so many strait hearts, cannot but produce such effects more and more, so as every indifferent minded man should be ready to say with father Abraham, "Take thou the right hand, and I will take the left." Let us not thus oppress, straiten, and afflict one another, but seeing there is a spacious land, the way to which is through the sea, we will end this difference in a day.

That I speak nothing about the bitter contention that hath been about religion, by writing, disputing, and inveighing earnestly one against another, the heat of which zeal, if it were turned against the rude barbarism of the heathens, it might do more good in a day than it hath done here in many years. Neither of the little love to the Gospel, and profit which is made by the preachers in most places, which might easily drive the zealous to the heathens who, no doubt, if they had but a drop of that knowledge which here flieth about the streets, would be filled with exceeding great joy and gladness, as that they would even pluck the kingdom of heaven by violence, and take it as it were, by force.

The greatest let[4] that is yet behind is the sweet fellowship of friends, and the satiety of bodily delights.

The last let.

But can there be two nearer friends almost than Abraham and Lot, or than Paul and Barnabas? And yet, upon as little occasions as we have here, they departed asunder, two of them being patriarchs of the church of old; the other the apostles of the church which is new, and their covenants were such as it seemeth might bind as much as any covenant between men at this day, and yet to avoid greater inconveniences they departed asunder.

Neither must men take so much thought for the flesh, as not to be pleased except they can pamper their bodies with variety of dainties. Nature is content with little, and health is much endangered by mixtures upon the stomach. The delights of the palate do often inflame the vital parts as the tongue setteth afire the whole body. Secondly, varieties here are not common to all, but many good men are glad to snap at a crust. The rent-taker lives on sweet morsels, but the rent-payer eats a dry crust often with watery eyes, and it is nothing to say what some one of a hundred hath, but what the bulk, body and commonalty

James 3:6.

4 hindrance

95

hath, which I warrant you is short enough.

And they also which now live so sweetly, hardly will their children attain to that privilege, but some circumventor or other will outstrip them, and make them sit in the dust, to which men are brought in one age, but cannot get out of it again in seven generations.

To conclude, without all partiality, the present consumption which groweth upon us here, whilst the land groaneth under so many close-fisted and unmerciful men, being compared with the easiness, plainness and plentifulness in living in those remote places, may quickly persuade any man to a liking of this course, and to practise a removal, which being done by honest, godly and industrious men, they shall there be right heartily welcome, but for other of dissolute and profane life, their rooms are better than their companies. For if here, where the Gospel hath been so long and plentifully taught, they are yet frequent in such vices as the heathen would shame to speak of, what will they be when there is less restraint in word and deed? My only suit to all men is, that whether they live there or here, they would learn to use this world as they used it not, keeping faith and a good conscience, both with God and men, that when the day of account shall come, they may come forth as good and fruitful servants, and freely be received, and enter into the joy of their Master.

R. C.[5]

FINIS

5 Presumably, Robert Cushman. See Introduction.

APPLEWOOD BOOKS
PUBLISHERS OF AMERICA'S LIVING PAST

*TIMELESS ADVICE AND ENTERTAINMENT
FROM AMERICANS WHO CAME BEFORE US*

❦

George Washington on Manners

Benjamin Franklin on Money

Lydia Maria Child on Raising Children

Henry David Thoreau on Walking

&

Many More Distinctive Classics

Now Available Again

❦

At finer bookstores

& gift shops or from:

APPLEWOOD BOOKS
P.O. Box 365
Bedford, MA 01730